Back Roads of Arizona

Colorado River toad

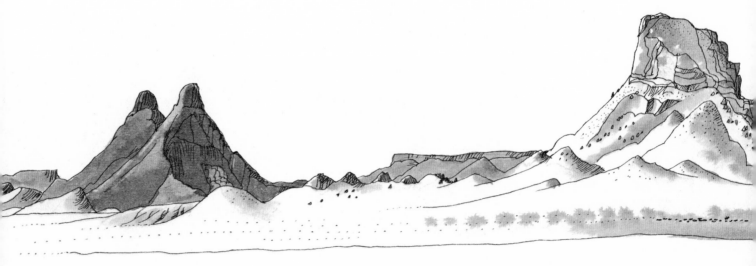

Indian country north of Holbrook

Books by Earl Thollander

BACK ROADS OF CALIFORNIA
BACK ROADS OF NEW ENGLAND
BARNS OF CALIFORNIA

Back Roads of Arizona
by Earl Thollander

INTRODUCTORY COMMENTARIES
by EDWARD ABBEY

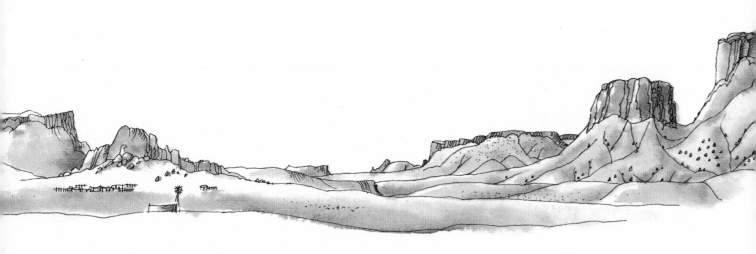

NORTHLAND PRESS / Flagstaff, Arizona

sore-eye poppy

FRONT COVER: Picacho Peak
BACK COVER: Weaver's Needle, Superstition Mountains

Copyright © 1978 by Earl Thollander
Introductory commentaries copyright © 1978 by Edward Abbey
All Rights Reserved
REVISED EDITION 1979
ISBN 0-87358-170-9 (cloth)
    0-87358-177-7 (paper)
Library of Congress Catalog Card Number 78-51122
Composed and Printed in the United States of America

*to Dave Clark
and Mel Lane...
who first
gave me
courage
to draw
a book*

Brittlebush

Contents

Legend for maps

  .   4   .   dots and numbers indicate
approximate mileage
between points

→ → → → arrows indicate my route
(routes may certainly be
reversed should you desire)

NORTH is always toward the top of the page

Geronimo Cave
near Fort Apache

Author's note

Most of the roads in this book were good enough for passenger cars at the time I traveled them. Some were not, and I have noted these on my maps. Please get local advice, however, when there is any question about present conditions of dirt and gravel roads. The maps should be most helpful in taking any of these back road trips. They are not to scale, however, due to the diversity in length of the various trips. The detailed county maps that I used are available, for a fee, from the Arizona Department of Transportation, 206 South 17th Avenue, Room 134, Phoenix, Arizona, 85007.

Gentian

Preface

What has impressed me most in my travels throughout Arizona are the great natural wonders and relics of antiquity still preserved for humankind to see.

The purpose of this book is to celebrate this fact, noting visually the fascination and charm of this unique part of America.

The hope is that this will inspire further regard and concern toward the preservation of both the history and natural beauty of Arizona.

I have tried to find roads that are enriching and exciting in themselves, agreeing with what photographer Josef Muench once said......"What matter where the road goes? The beauty is in the journey."

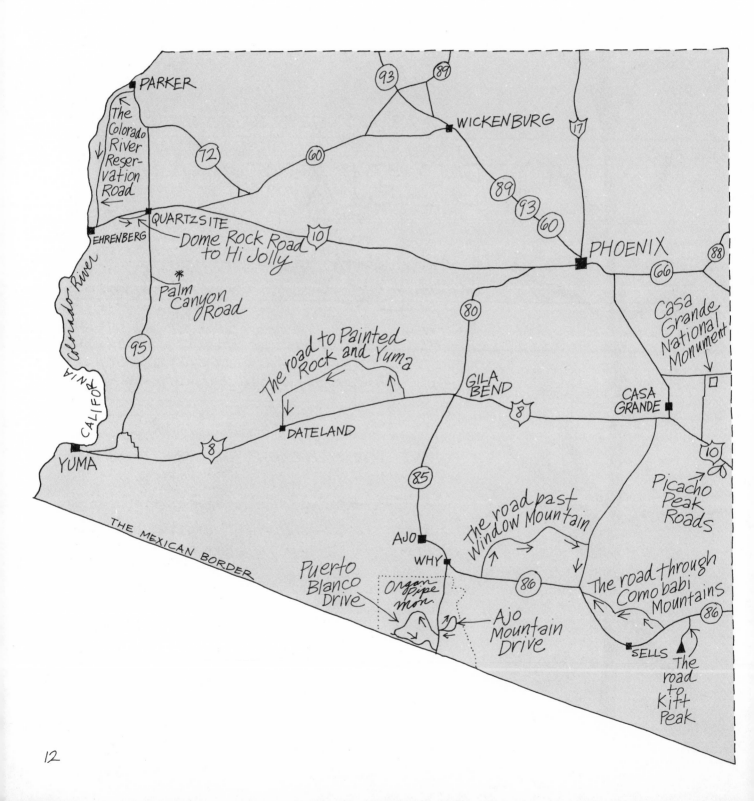

PARKER

93   89

WICKENBURG

17

The
Colorado
River
Reser-
vation
Road

12   60

89
93
60

QUARTZSITE

EHRENBERG

Dome Rock Road
to Hi Jolly

10

PHOENIX

66

88

Palm
Canyon
Road

Colorado River

95

80

Casa
Grande
National
Monument

The road to Painted
Rock and Yuma

GILA
BEND

8

CASA
GRANDE

CALIFORNIA

DATELAND

10

YUMA

8

85

Picacho
Peak
Roads

THE MEXICAN BORDER

AJO

WHY

The road past
Window Mountain

86

The road through
Como babi
Mountains

86

Puerto
Blanco
Drive

Organ
Pipe
Mon.

Ajo
Mountain
Drive

SELLS

The
road
to
Kitt
Peak

Southwestern Arizona

Nothing could demonstrate better the superiority of art to technology than these simple, charming, evocative and completely accurate drawings by Mr. Thollander. Compared to this supple work by a man who can feel, as well as see and draw, even the best photography seems—at least to me—like something cold and shallow, empty and useless. Photography describes; art contemplates, expresses, communicates. Much as I admire good photography—the work, say, of Philip Hyde or Ansel Adams—there is, even in the best of it, the lack of something vital, i.e., vitality. Life. Photography can record and document with uncanny precision; but between the object and the subject falls the invisible barrier of a mechanical technique, devoid of human mediation. The camera, the film, the scene and lighting can all be manipulated, controlled—up to a point. But at the crucial moment the outcome is determined not by human thought or feeling but by the outside agencies of light, time, chemistry. The best photograph is only a substitute for the true thing; an artificial eye recording, with the shutter's blink, an abstract and abstracted fragment from the seamless flow of reality. A work of art, on the other hand, whether quick sketch or patient painting, presents us not only with a representation of the world outside our heads but also with a picture of the mind and personality of the artist himself. A composition rather than merely an image. If successful, a work of art does more than hold a mirror up to nature; it becomes an addition to nature. A photograph is of value only in its reference to something beyond itself; it is but a Platonic shadow of the real world *out there*. A work of art, however, *is* the real thing—a world of its own.

Saguaro

The Colorado Indian Reservation road

Another way to travel south from Parker was to go through the Indian Reservation. I first stopped in Parker to see the Chemehuevi basket collection at the Colorado River Indian Tribes Museum.

I sketched a Mojave effigy doll while an Indian attendant swept the museum floor nearby. The dust made me sneeze!

From Parker the trip south affords views of cotton and hay croplands. Sheep graze in the green pastureland.

The three mountains, Avi Suguilla, Avi Carotat and Avi Vatai are the rough northern boundaries of the Colorado River Indian Reservation.

mountains along the Colorado River

avi Carotat

Mojave effigy doll

15

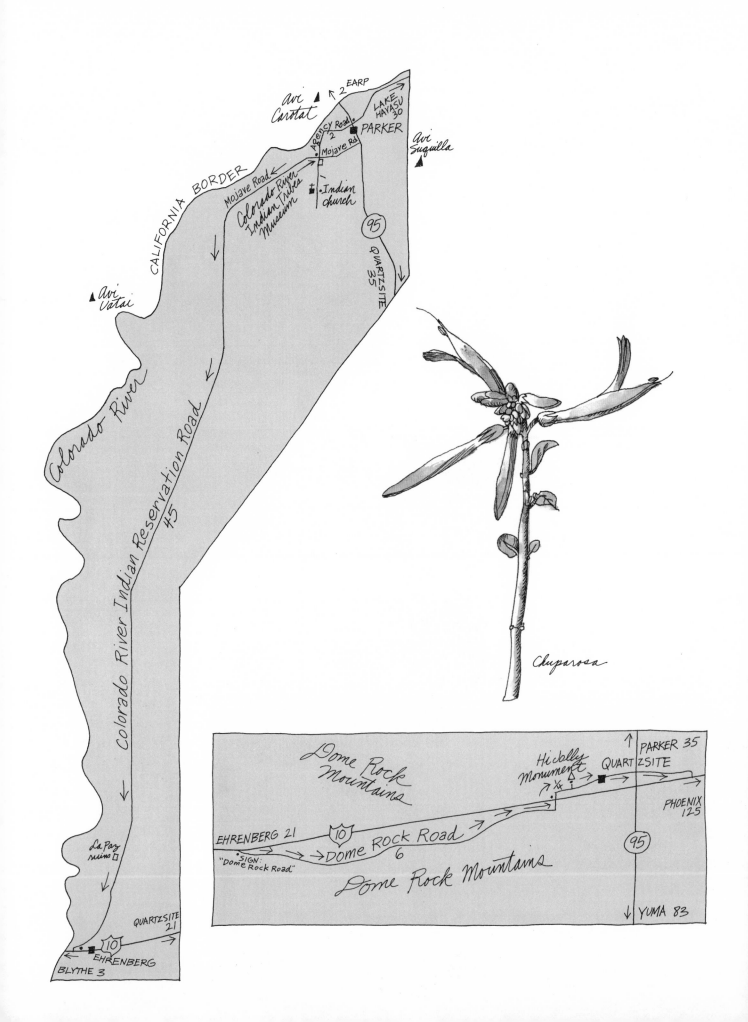

EARP
↑ 2

Avi Carotat ▲

PARKER

Agency Road
2

Mojave Rd.

LAKE
HAYASU
30

Avi Suquilla ▲

Mojave Road ←

Colorado River Indian Tribes Museum

† • Indian church

CALIFORNIA BORDER

(95)

QUARTZSITE
35

▲ *Avi Vatai*

Colorado River

Colorado River Indian Reservation Road
45

Chuparosa

La Paz ruins □

QUARTZSITE
21

(10)

EHRENBERG

BLYTHE 3

Dome Rock Mountains

Hi Jolly
Monument

↑ PARKER 35

QUARTZSITE

EHRENBERG 21

(10) *Dome Rock Road*
6

SIGN:
"Dome Rock Road"

PHOENIX
125

(95)

Dome Rock Mountains

↓ YUMA 83

Dome Rock Road to Hi Jolly

Going east from Ehrenberg I turned off the highway at Dome Rock Road and then relaxed driving along the old road past the Dome Rock Mountains.

I crossed over the main highway to Quartzsite to see the unusual Hi Jolly Camel Driver's Tomb. It was Jefferson Davis who had the idea of importing camels for freighting and communication in the arid Southwest. Haiji Ali, or "Hi Jolly" spelled American style, came with the camels from Syria as caretaker in 1856.

The animals were worthy, but the experiment was finally dropped. The camels, without jobs, stayed in Quartzsite, adding a bizarre and colorful aspect to the town.

THE LAST CAMP
OF
HI JOLLY
BORN SOMEWHERE IN SYRIA
ABOUT 1828
DIED AT QUARTZSITE
DECEMBER 16, 1902
CAME TO THIS COUNTRY
FEBRUARY 10, 1856

CAMELDRIVER- PACKER
SCOUT - OVER THIRTY
YEARS A FAITHFUL AID
TO THE U.S. GOVERMENT

ARIZONA
HIGHWAY DEPARTMENT
1935

Hi Jolly Monument, Quartzsite

Castle Dome Peak,
Kofa National Wildlife Reserve

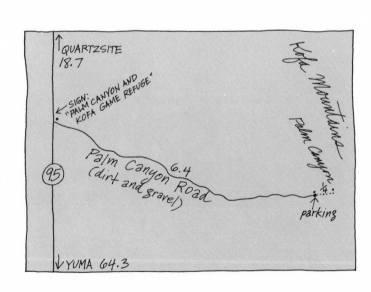

↑ QUARTZSITE
18.7

← SIGN:
"PALM CANYON AND
KOFA GAME REFUGE"

Kofa Mountains

Palm Canyon

⑨⑤   Palm Canyon Road   6.4
      (dirt and gravel)

parking

↓ YUMA 64.3

Palm Canyon Road

The road was gravel and passenger cars had to go slowly in several places or bottoms would be scraped. The view toward Kofa Mountains and the National Game Refuge became more dramatic as I drove east across the desert.

There was a place to park and a one-quarter mile trail up to Palm Canyon. I had the religious feeling of entering a magnificent natural cathedral as I hiked into the canyon ahead. It came as a surprise when I first glimpsed the palms vertically arranged up a narrow canyon. Walking back again the ancient landscape stretched out endless and green in a lavish display of desert plants and shrubs. Along the path bright yellow brittlebush flowers were blooming as were purple wild heliotrope and red chuparosa.

Palm Canyon

21

Petroglyphs—Painted Rocks

The road to Painted Rocks and Yuma

Black "rock varnish," formed on the originally light-colored rock surface over eons of time, has made the boulders at Painted Rocks suitable surfaces for ancient petroglyph carvers.

The ranger on duty here had a constant job keeping children from climbing over the glyphs and threatening their eventual obliteration.

Some rocks had been defaced as early as 1815 by a certain "S. N. C." and as late as 1957 by "Max G.," however it was a joy to see the many undefiled and gayly decorated ones.

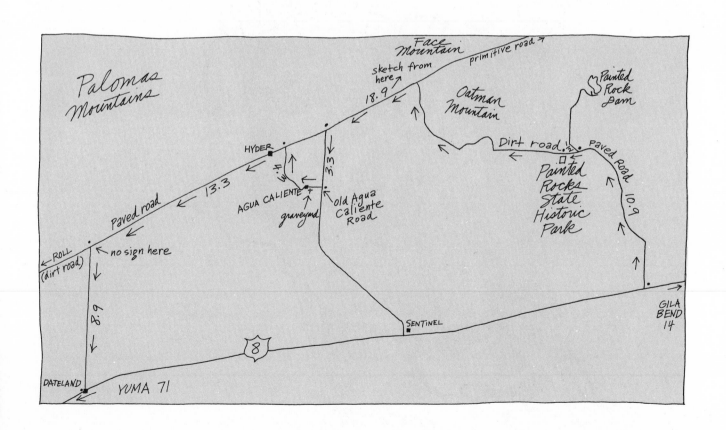

Petroglyphs,
Painted Rocks

ROSA C SANCHEZ
18_? APRIL.15.1915

agua Caliente
headstone

The back road from Painted Rocks was dirt
a large part of the way. Along this byway you
will see Montezuma's head resting peacefully
on the horizon. It is remarkable that a
mountain can become a face.

Face Mountain

Territorial Prison
State Historic Park

A stop in Yuma

   At Yuma the Territorial Prison State Historic
Park was a busy place with a major highway
  and an active railroad passing directly by
the old jail. The Colorado River flows by
  quietly on the north end of this colorful
location.   I walked up to the main guard
  station from where the only entrance to the
  old jail could be watched.
           The museum has pictures of former
inmates and momentos of the time from 1876
to 1909 when the prison was in operation. The
old jail cells, too, were available to see.
     I sat on the thick lawn in front of the main
entrance, also called "Sallyport."

I would venture to say no lush palm and cactus garden graced the entrance in the old days.

Agua Caliente headstone

27

Puerto Blanco Drive

This was a 51-mile dirt road within Organ Pipe National Monument. It afforded me a good look at a thriving desert community of plants — and some of the wildlife.

While sitting quietly at Quitobaquito pond I observed many varieties of birds. Over 180 species have been identified at this desert oasis.

The Ajo Mountain Drive was a 21-mile dirt road with great desert and mountain views. There was hiking at Arch Canyon or along Bull Pasture Trail. I spent the night at Gringo Pass, also called Lukeville, near Organ Pipe National Monument on the Mexican border.

Ajo Range, Organ Pipe
Cactus National Monument

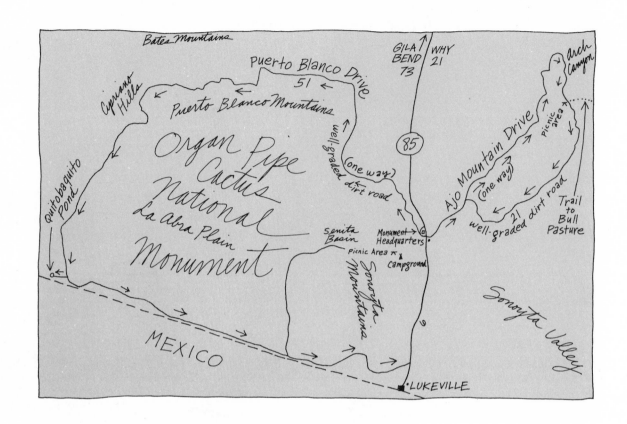

Bates Mountains

Puerto Blanco Drive
51

GILA BEND 73   WHY 21

Cipriano Hills

Puerto Blanco Mountains

Organ Pipe
Cactus
National
La Abra Plain
Monument

Arch Canyon

Ajo Mountain Drive

picnic area

85

(one way)

well-graded dirt road

Quitobaquito Pond

Senita Basin

Monument Headquarters

Picnic Area π
Campground

Sonoyta Mountains

(one way)

21
well-graded dirt road

Trail to Bull Pasture

Sonoyta Valley

MEXICO

•LUKEVILLE

Goldenbush

The road past Window Mountain

This was a vast Indian reservation I traveled. The world seemed all sky and horizon in Papago land.
At Hickiwan there was a bright, white little church.
In Vaya Chin I sketched a Papago home built with ocotillo, mesquite, saguaro spines and caliche. Caliche is the fine mud, rich in calcium, that is plastered to both roof and sides of dwellings.
My audience for the drawing was four dogs, one of which barked at me without stopping, rousing the other three to token barking from time to time.

Papago home, Vaya Chin

Past Vaya Chin I got my first view of Window Mountain's "window". Farther along the road two "windows" may be seen. This area was also the site of Ventana Cave where evidence of human habitation dating back 10,000 years has been found. Some of this evidence can be seen handsomely displayed at the Arizona State Museum in Tucson.

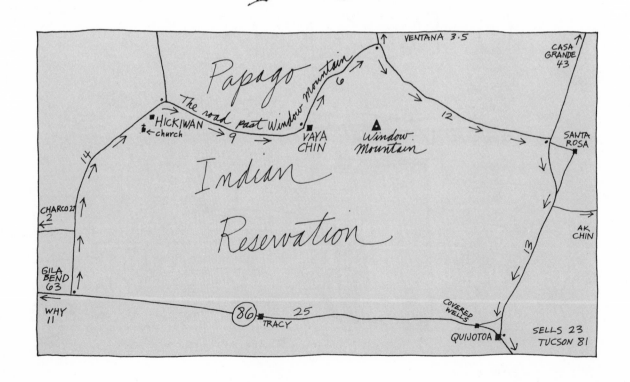

Window Mountain

CABABI

The road through Comobabi Mountains

A desert dirt road went to Sikul Hamatk, Cobabi and Comobabi. These were quiet little Papago villages, elegant in their simplicity. I sketched Cobabi's nicely proportioned church and also an adobe corral made with mesquite logs.

The church at Cobabi

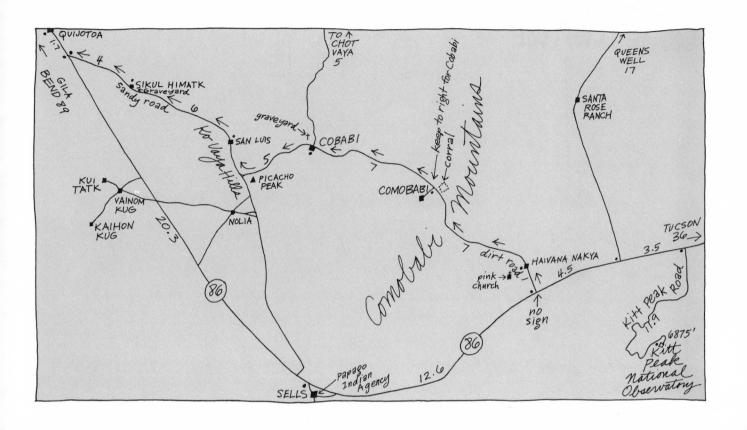

Map labels:

QUIJOTOA
1.7
4
GILA BEND 89
SIKUL HIMATK
graveyard
sandy road
6
Ko Vaya Hills
San Luis
graveyard
5
TO CHOT VAYA 5
COBABI
keep to right for Cobabi
corral
7
Comobabi Mountains
QUEENS WELL 17
SANTA ROSE RANCH
KUI TATK
VAINOM KUG
20.3
NOLIA
PICACHO PEAK
COMOBABI
KAIHON KUG
Comobabi
dirt road
7
HAIVANA NAKYA
4.5
TUCSON 36
3.5
Kitt Peak Road
1.9
pink church
no sign
6875'
Kitt Peak National Observatory
86
86
12.6
SELLS
Papago Indian Agency

Papagos are people of the soil with the special knowledge to operate farms that depend on infrequent rain.

A Papago cowboy emerged from the Palo Verde trees and cactus surrounding the village of Cobabi and quietly rode by as I sketched.

Later, two smiling Indian girls rode by in tandem on their horse.

Corral at Cobabi

These villages are private places.
 It is best not to disturb their
tranquility, so one must continue on.
 The Cobabi cemetery crosses
gleamed white on the gently
rolling slope opposite the road
 from the town.

38

The road to Kitt Peak

Kitt Peak, in legend, is the favorite dwelling
place of I-I'Toy, Papago protector.
Today it is also the home of the Kitt Peak
National Observatory, leased from the
Papago tribe. Views from the top were
overwhelming in their magnitude. There was
a walking tour of the various facilities
including the unique solar observatory.

Kitt Peak

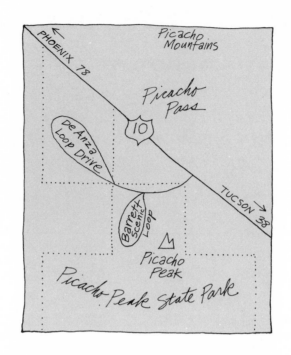

Picacho Peak roads

Picacho Peak has been a landmark for Indians, Spanish colonists, frontier military units, Butterfield Overland Mail stagecoaches and lone prospectors. This area was also the stage for Arizona's one and only Civil War confrontation, "The Battle of Picacho", April 15, 1862.

The peak remains a prominent landmark today in the great Sonoran desert with a highway and railroad passing on the plain below.

Two short loop roads took me through the park. I sketched looking into the morning sun while a cactus wren and a curved-bill thrasher entertained me with sounds of scratching, fluttering and chirping.

Picacho Peak

41

The road to Casa Grande Ruins

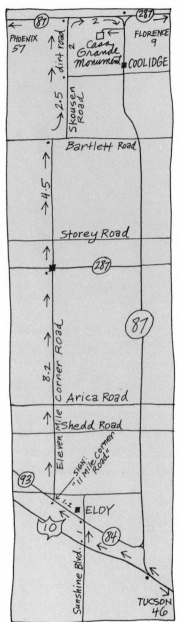

I took a back road to Casa Grande National Monument, a quiet road through farm country. Casa Grande with its great protective "hat" appeared on the horizon, and I soon joined the many visitors at the marvelous ruin.

The roof over the "big house" was erected in 1932. It is an anachronism but, of course, essential to its preservation. It was no problem to leave the roof out of my drawing, one of the advantages of sketching.

Casa Grande was named by the Jesuit priest, Father Kino, in 1694. He reported that the building, even then, was in ruins. It was probably built around 1350 A.D. by the Hohokam Indians. Casa Grande is not a typical Indian structure at all, and its use is unexplained to this day.

The four-story earth building may have been a ceremonial ediface, an ancient astronomical observatory, or, can you guess its purpose?

Casa Grande

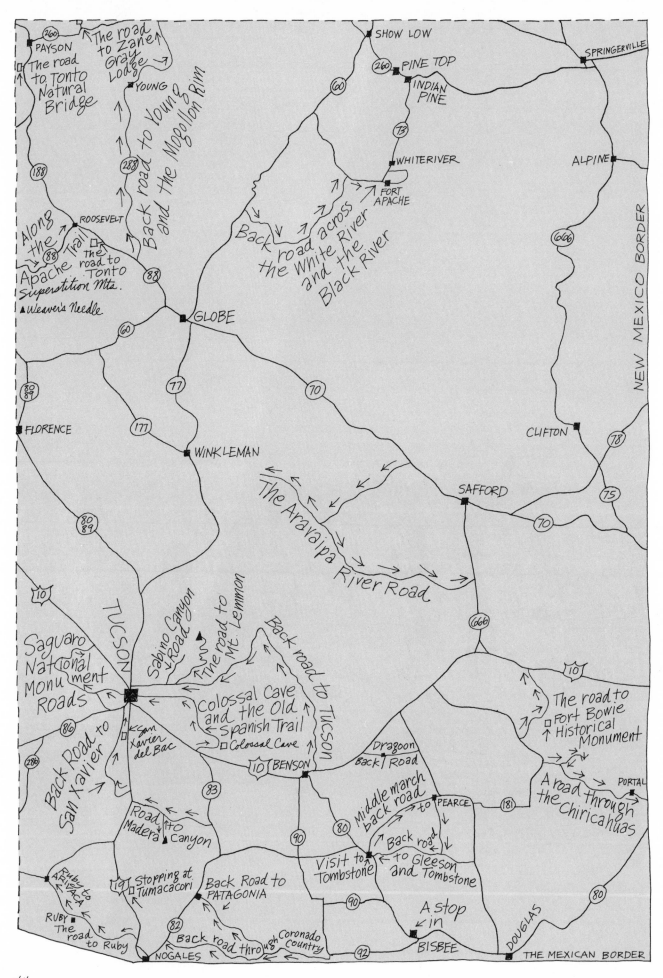

260
PAYSON
The road to Zane Gray Lodge
The road to Tonto Natural Bridge
YOUNG
SHOW LOW
SPRINGERVILLE
260
PINE TOP
60
INDIAN PINE
73
Back road to Young and the Mogollon Rim
288
188
WHITERIVER
ALPINE
Along the Apache Trail
88
ROOSEVELT
The road to Tonto Superstition Mts.
88
▲ Weaver's Needle
60
Back road across the White River and the Black River
FORT APACHE
666
GLOBE
77
70
NEW MEXICO BORDER
80
89
171
FLORENCE
WINKLEMAN
CLIFTON
78
The Aravaipa River Road.
SAFFORD
75
80
89
70
666
10
TUCSON
Saguaro National Monument Roads
Sabino Canyon Road
The road to Mt. Lemmon
Back road to Tucson
10
The road to Fort Bowie Historical Monument
86
Colossal Cave and the Old Spanish Trail
☐ Colossal Cave
Dragoon Back Road
A road through the Chiricahuas
PORTAL
Back Road to San Xavier
☐ San Xavier del Bac
286
10 BENSON
181
83
Middle march back road
to PEARCE
Road to Madera Canyon
80
Back road to Gleeson and Tombstone
90
Visit to Tombstone
Ruby to ARIVACA
19 Stopping at Tumacacori
Back Road to PATAGONIA
A stop in
RUBY The road to Ruby
82
90
BISBEE
DOUGLAS
80
Back road through Coronado Country
92
THE MEXICAN BORDER
NOGALES

Southeastern Arizona

We need more back roads. Not so many front roads. I am absolutely in favor of stripping the asphalt from most of our highways in America—and elsewhere—reprocessing the stuff and recycling it into something useful: roofing material, perhaps, or gasoline, or medicines, or simply reducing it all to liquid form and pouring it back down into the holes from which we extracted it in the first place. I see no evidence anywhere that technology and the industrial way of life have added one quantum of freedom, beauty or dignity to human life. In what way, for example, is the existence of a factory worker, a store clerk, a truck driver or a school teacher superior to that of the buffalo-hunting Plains Indians? For every point of improvement in the lives of the former I can show a corresponding loss. Industrialism has not elevated our standard of living; it has merely increased our rate of consumption. This rapid, efficient and self-defeating exploitation of Nature supplies us with the means to support our rapidly expanding human numbers; but after a brief 200 years we are already confronted with the specter of diminishing resources, leading toward conflict, war, famine, plague—Nature's customary response to man's irrational greed. What is the answer to this dilemma? A voluntary or involuntary return to the Age of Stone? A blind, trusting surrender of our fate to the engineers and technocrats? Or is there another way, a middle way, the way of reason, sense and common sense, an end to our war of conquest against the natural world? An incurable optimist, I think there is that better way. Travel the back roads at an easy pace, look at the scene not through the midget eye of a camera but with your whole being, and you will see what I mean.

Desert Marigold

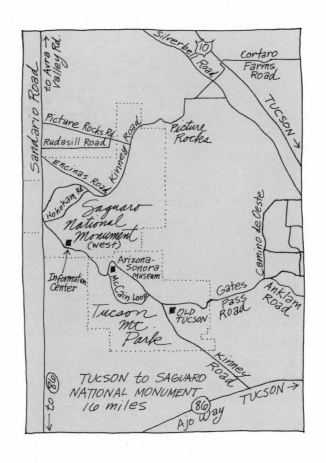

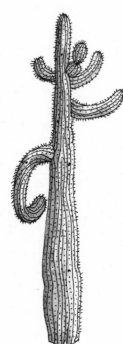

Saguaro National Monument Roads

In the monument west of Tucson
I sketched a road lined with giant
saguaros and Apache Peak in the
background. This trip was
accompanied by a visit to the
Arizona Sonora Desert Museum,
the home of an exceptional
display of birds, animals, insects
and plants of the desert —
including the strange
Boojum tree.

Saguaros and Apache Peak

Colossal Cave and the Old Spanish Trail

The stone building at the entrance to Colossal Cave blends in with the landscape looking a bit like a monastery in a strange land. After a visit to the cave I drove through the Saguaro National Monument east of Tucson via the Old Spanish Trail.

Along this road the saguaros seemed larger and healthier than any I had ever seen.

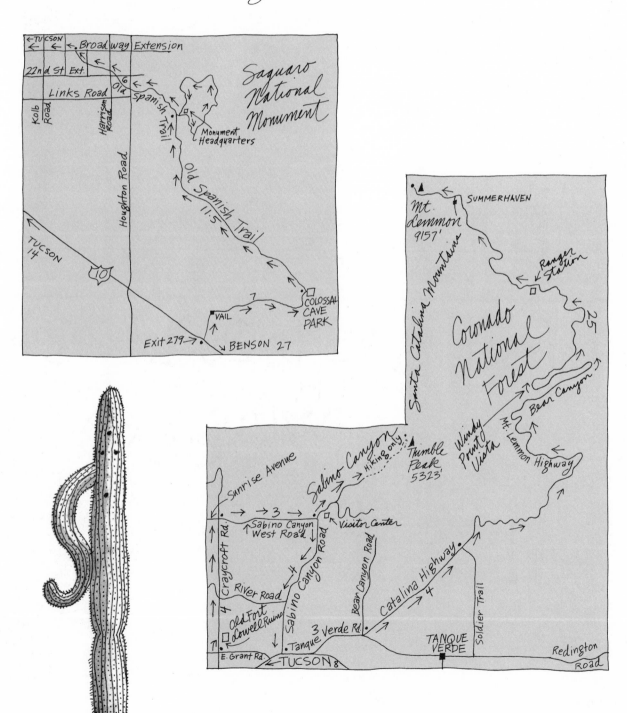

The road to Mount Lemmon

Lone piñon pine

Mt. Lemmon is 9,157 feet high yet
the summit was only 40 miles from
Tucson. There is skiing in the winter-
time on the peak. It was interesting
to note the zonal changes that occured
as I drove from the desert floor
through oak woodlands to juniper,
piñon and ponderosa pine forests.
A mile or so north of Windy Point I
sketched a piñon pine seemingly
growing out of rock.

Sabino Canyon Road

On the south face of the Santa Catalina Mountains, Sabino Canyon was an oasis with a flowing creek — and a good place to hike and picnic.

Going by way of Craycroft Road I was able to visit the ruins of Fort Lowell and, on a warm day, enjoy there the luxurious shade of its great lane of cottonwood trees.

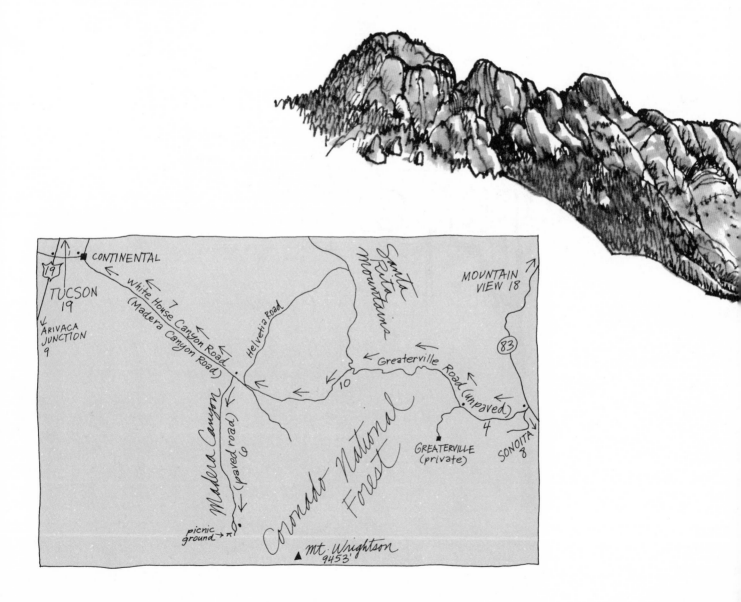

Road to Madera Canyon

Madera Canyon in the Santa Rita Mountains was another place to picnic, hike or bird-watch.   It was a cold day in February when I sketched 9,453-foot Mt. Wrightson from the canyon floor. Atop the mountain drifts of snow clung in crevices of rock, and with heavy mists beginning to obscure the peak, I completed my drawing.

Mt. Wrightson from Madera Canyon

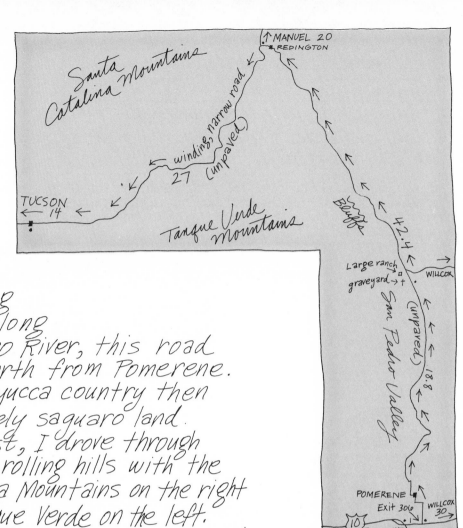

Back road
to
Tucson

Past ranches
  and through
  gulleys, noting
  the bluffs along
the San Pedro River, this road
proceeded north from Pomerene.
  Soap tree yucca country then
became stately saguaro land.
  Turning west, I drove through
picturesque, rolling hills with the
Santa Catalina Mountains on the right
  and the Tanque Verde on the left.
  When finally a descent was made
toward Tucson I was rewarded with a
sweeping view of the entire Tucson area.

Desert Ruin

Back road to San Xavier

San Xavier was a lovely Spanish Mission (1783) to
see on the Papago Indian Reservation. From the
south a back road approach to the Mission began at
Duval Mine Road. I went west toward the Amenex
Mining area but stopped at the Visitor Viewpoint to
see the immense open-pit copper mining
operation. It was truly an astonishing sight!
        To draw the Mission in its setting, I
crossed the Santa Cruz River and looked back.
The hills behind San Xavier del Bac were very dark
and the white Mission glowed as if lit from within.
        Along the banks of the river an Indian
farmer pushed his wheelbarrow,
cows grazed, and the sun
moved across the sky and
set behind the hills.

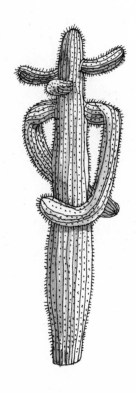

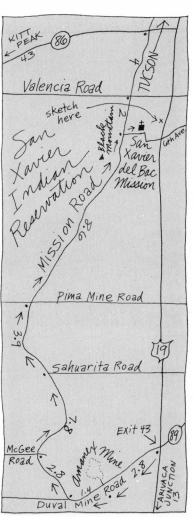

Mission San Xavier del Bac

The Aravaipa Creek Road

I took a dirt back road around the Pinaleno Mountains into the Aravaipa Valley, stopping along the road at Klondyke to sketch the old post office.

I sat sketching by the dirt road. Waving in a friendly fashion, farmers occasionally drove by leaving behind billowing clouds of dust.

The most beautiful part of the trip was to follow the Aravaipa River as far as I could. Peppery watercress grew in the stream and giant Fremont Cottonwood and Arizona Sycamore flourished.

You may get permission to enter the George Whittell Wildlife Refuge at the end of the road by asking in Klondyke, however the gate is usually open and you are welcome, I imagine, if you mean no harm to the wildlife or landscape.

It was a tranquil and spiritually refreshing place to be. It was here that I saw my first bobcat in the wild.

The return trip skirted the Pinaleno Mountains on their south side. And I enjoyed seeing the decorative soap tree yuccas along the way.

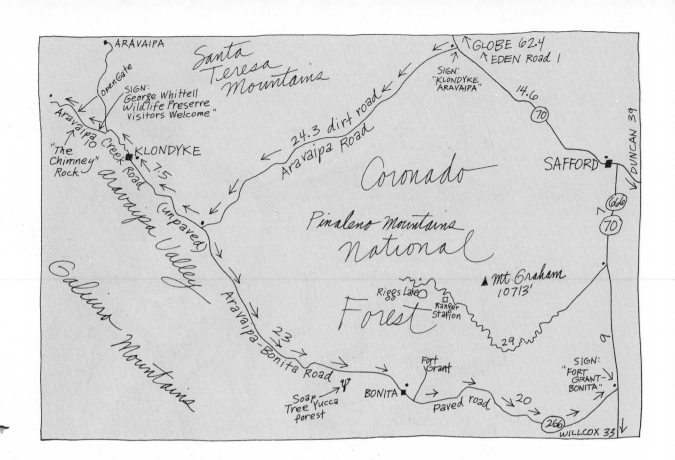

ARAVAIPA

Santa Teresa Mountains

Open Gate

SIGN:
"George Whittell
Wildlife Preserve
Visitors Welcome"

Aravaipa Creek Road

"The Chimney" Rock

KLONDYKE

7.5

10

(unpaved)

Aravaipa Valley

24.3 dirt road

Aravaipa Road

GLOBE 62.4
EDEN Road 1

SIGN:
"KLONDYKE-
ARAVAIPA"

14.6

(70)

SAFFORD

DUNCAN 39

(666)

(70)

Coronado

Pinaleno Mountains

National

Galiuro Mountains

Aravaipa-Bonita Road

23

Soap Tree Yucca forest

BONITA

Riggs Lake

▲ Mt. Graham
10713'

Ranger Station

Forest

Fort Grant

29

σ

SIGN:
"FORT
GRANT-
BONITA"

Paved road

20

(266)

WILLCOX 33

Klondyke, Arizona.
U.S. POST OFFICE

CLOSED

U.S. POST OFFICE

58

The Chimney,
Aravaipa Canyon

The road to Fort Bowie

Driving on a dirt road six miles to Apache Pass, a 1½-mile hike then brought me to the fort ruins. I saw the post graveyard and the historic Apache spring along the way.

The first Fort Bowie was established in 1862 to subdue the elusive Apache. (The Apache had, incidentally, used the Pass and the spring since the 1600's.) A second fort was built in 1868. Amongst its ruins I sat in what was once the bar of the old fort's Trade Post.

The sketch through the doorway looks out at "Helen's Dome," named for an influential officer's wife.

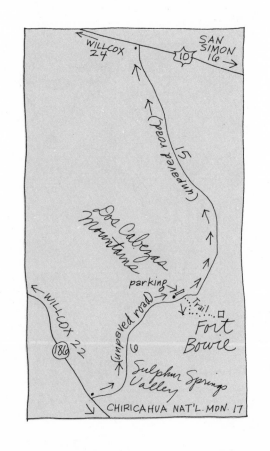

WILLCOX 24

SAN SIMON 16 →

10

(5 unpaved road)

Dos Cabezas Mountains

parking →

Trail....□

Fort Bowie

← WILLCOX 22

186

(unpaved road) 6

Sulphur Springs Valley

CHIRICAHUA NAT'L. MON. 17

View from the bar,
Fort Bowie

61

Fulton's find

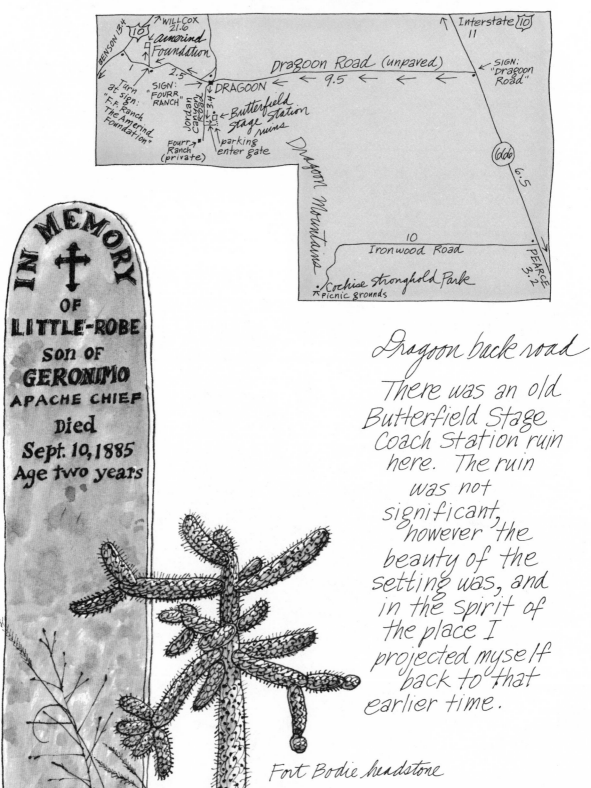

On the map:

WILLCOX 21.6

BENSON 13.4

10

Amerind Foundation

2.5

Interstate 10

11

SIGN: "Dragoon Road"

Dragoon Road (unpaved) 9.5

Turn at sign: "F.F. Ranch The Amerind Foundation"

SIGN: "FOURR RANCH"

Jordan Canyon Road

3.4

↓DRAGOON

Butterfield Stage Station ruins

Dragoon Mountains

666

6.5

PEARCE 3.2

Fourr Ranch (private)

parking enter gate

10

Ironwood Road

Cochise Stronghold Park

picnic grounds

Dragoon back road

There was an old Butterfield Stage Coach Station ruin here. The ruin was not significant, however the beauty of the setting was, and in the spirit of the place I projected myself back to that earlier time.

IN MEMORY OF LITTLE-ROBE SON OF GERONIMO APACHE CHIEF Died Sept. 10, 1885 Age two years

Fort Bodie headstone

I surveyed the vast valley floor and it seemed unchanged since the days of stagecoach travel.

A significant collection of Indian artifacts by the Amerind Foundation is near Dragoon. The Foundation had no regular staff member to conduct tours so reservations were necessary to see the great collection.

There were regular tours saturday and sunday at 10:30 and 1:30, telephone 602/586 3003, or write The Amerind Foundation Inc., Dragoon, Arizona. In the museum I sketched the modest little jar discovered in the Mingus Mountains in 1913 by Amerind's founder William Shirley Fulton.

Mountain spirit headdress

His find so intrigued him that he decided to begin the extensive work of creating what is now the Amerind Foundation.

I also sketched a mask and headdress worn by Apaches to impersonate a mountain spirit during girl's "coming of age" ceremonies. The four day rite would dramatise the triumph of good over evil.

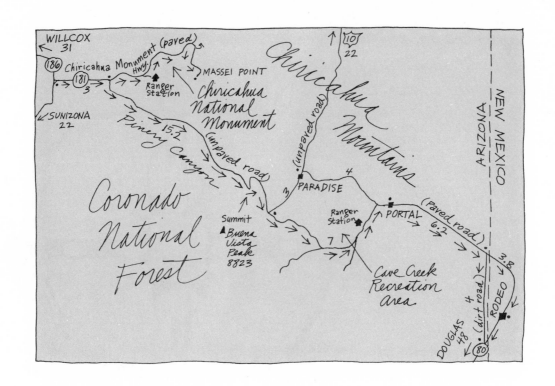

WILLCOX 31
186 Chiricahua Monument (paved)
181 Chiricahua Monument Hwy.
3
MASSEI POINT
Ranger Station
SUNIZONA 22
Pinery Canyon
15.2
(unpaved road)
Chiricahua National Monument
Chiricahua Mountains
(unpaved road)
10
22
ARIZONA
NEW MEXICO
Coronado National Forest
Summit
Buena Vista Peak 8823
PARADISE
4
3
Ranger Station
7
PORTAL
(paved road)
6.2
Cave Creek Recreation area
3.8
RODEO
DOUGLAS 48
(dirt road)
4
80

A road through the Chiricahuas

The erosional action that created the
Chiricahua National Monument was an artistic
one indeed. Rows of spires, turrets and
battlements stood like pieces in an enormous
chess set. Nature had fashioned sculptural
masterpieces for us to enjoy
in perpetuity.
The back road over the mountains
south and east of the Monument was dirt
and gravel, passable if winter's snows
were gone from the topmost pass.
The trip was immensely rewarding
with deep shadows accenting richly
colored views near Portal.

Chiricahua
National
Monument

Bisbee

A stop in Bisbee

One of the most colorful towns in Arizona must be Bisbee with its atmosphere of a mining town of the 1890's or early 1900's. Homes cling to narrow canyon walls in seemingly impossible situations to reach, until one explores the town and observes the network of narrow roads and long stairways that connect them all. The mining boom days are gone and one would wish that Bisbee, to keep its historic look, could be protected as a National Monument.

Schiefflin's gun

Visit to Tombstone

The years of Tombstone's existence
as a successful mining center were
short. But in 1881, with 10,000 population and
millions of dollars in silver being taken
from the surrounding area, the Arizona
legislature not only created Cochise County
but decided to build the new county's
courthouse in town. It was still the most
elegant building in Tombstone to me, and it
housed all sorts of antiques and artifacts
telling of the colorful past. I sketched
Ed Schiefflin's 1860 .44 Henry rifle, "the
most treasured antique in the museum,"
I was told. It was Ed who really inspired
the name for the town. He was warned that
with the Apaches on the warpath all he might
find prospecting in this area would be
his tombstone. Instead, he found silver
and named his claim "Tombstone" in
remembrance of the prediction.
The town's name was subsequently
changed from Goose Flats to Tombstone.

The Courthouse

Space heater, Pearce store

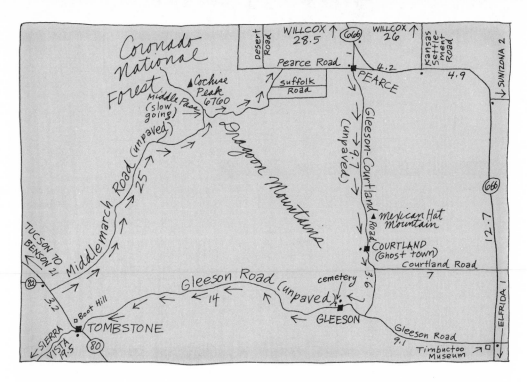

Middlemarch back road to Pearce

This road went through the Dragoon Mountains near Tombstone. The trip was best taken in this direction due to some steep turns on the other side of Middle Pass. Arizona history and lore, stories heard and read of Indians, miners and soldiers came to mind in this place of rugged beauty.

In Pearce the old store looked to me much like it might have in 1893 when, so it is said, the town was wilder and more desperate than Tombstone.

I sketched the practical old space heater with its extended stovepipe through the ceiling.

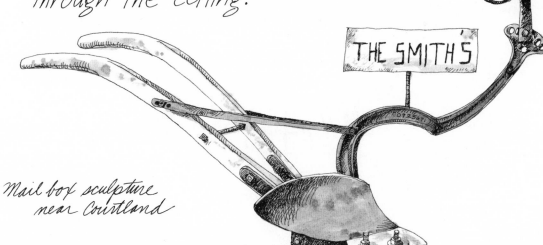

Mail box sculpture
near Courtland

Ghost Town back road to Tombstone

From Pearce I traveled on a dirt road past ghostly remnants of the town of Courtland scattered among the rolling hills. At Gleeson there was a partially revived ghost town. The arched entryway of the Gleeson school still stood on the south side of town.

As a collector of drawings of inventive, bizarre, humorous or otherwise interesting headstones, I sketched these two at Gleeson cemetery.

YEE WEE
BORN IN CHINA
I SEE YOU TOMORROW
FEB. 20, 1968

Back road
through Coronado country

From Montezuma Pass there is a
grand view of the San Pedro Valley
where Coronado traveled in June, 1540,
with a party of soldiers, priests and
Mexican-Indians. His was the
first major exploration by Europeans into
the American southwest.
   I continued on this back road through
inspiring natural scenery all the way to Nogales.

View from Montezuma Pass

Albert Gattrell home, 1898, Sunnyside

Back road to Patagonia

Instead of going toward Nogales you may also turn right at Washington Camp, just past Duquesne, and drive to Patagonia. This road passes the ghost town of Mowry. The town site is unmarked, but if you look sharply enough you will see its adobe ruins among the growing forest of oak and juniper trees. I sketched as cowboys rode by in winter sheepskins. It was a sunny but cold day in February.

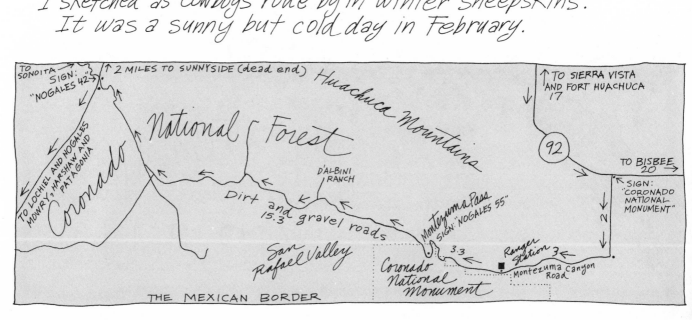

Ghost town ruin, Mowry

1e0 0.
DE AVRIL.
ANGELES.
SOTO.

There was a colorful roadside
cemetery at the site of the old
mining town of Harshaw.
Little else was in evidence
memorializing the past of
this ghostly place.

ghost town
cemetery

Tumacacori

Stopping at Tumacacori

Tumacacori, founded by Franciscan priests, stands in melancholy splendor, a reminder of the Spanish colonial endeavor in southern Arizona. Building probably began around 1800, but in 1821 Mexico won independence from Spain and the mission was abandoned. A traveler in 1849 wrote, "The walls of the church still stand, no roof, and only the upright piece of the cross. It looks desolate indeed."

The site of the old presidio, Arizona's oldest Spanish settlement, was at Tubac, a pleasant stop for tourists three miles north of Tumacacori.

The road to Ruby

There were interesting peaks and buttes along this road. Just past Pena Canyon were views of Castle Rock. Later there was Thumb Rock and then Montana Peak at Ruby.

The ghost town of Ruby awaited the ravages of time in its mountain setting. Privately owned, it was not available for exploration, however the lonesome old town was visible from the road.

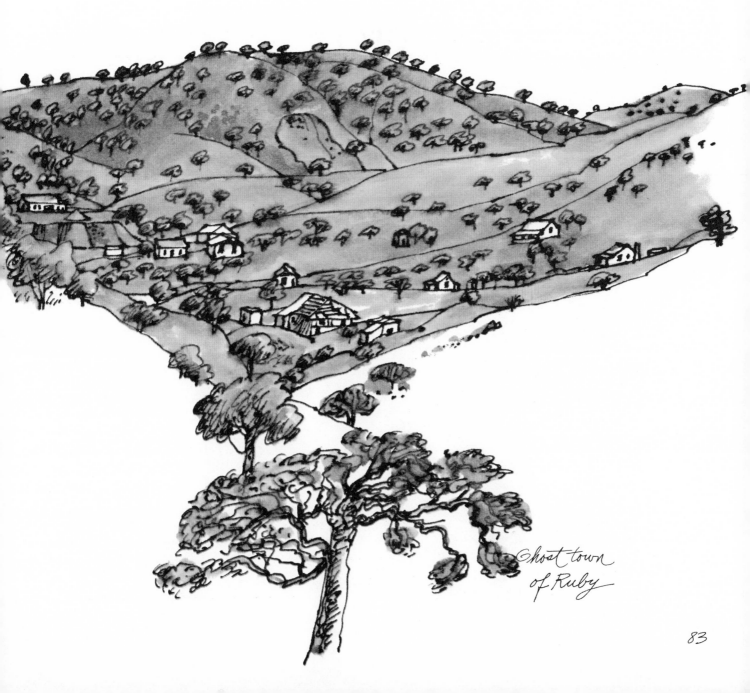

Ghost town
of Ruby

Baboquivari from Arivaca

Ruby to Arivaca

This very scenic back road went to Arivaca bringing closer and closer views of the gigantic 7,730-foot mountain of stone, Baboquivari Peak, in Papago Indian land.

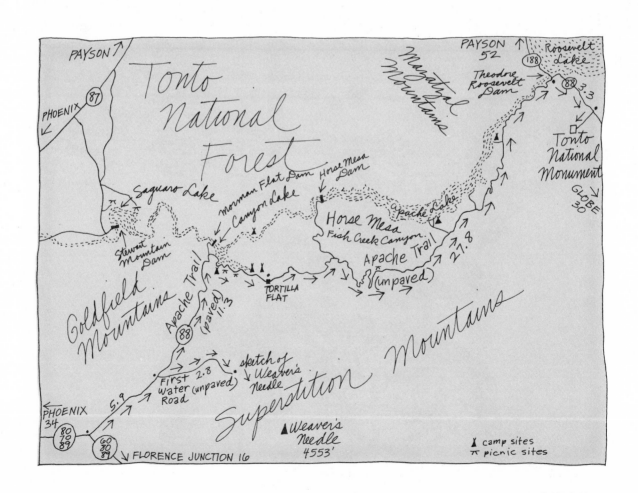

PAYSON ↗

87

PHOENIX

Tonto National Forest

PAYSON ↑ 52   Roosevelt Lake

188   3.3

Mazatzal Mountains

Theodore Roosevelt Dam

88

Saguaro Lake   Morman Flat Dam   Horse Mesa Dam

Canyon Lake

Horse Mesa   Apache Lake

Fish Creek Canyon

Tonto National Monument

GLOBE 30

Stewart Mountain Dam

Goldfield Mountains

Apache Trail (paved) 11.3

TORTILLA FLAT

Apache Trail (unpaved) 21.8

88

First 2.8 Water Road (unpaved)

sketch of Weaver's Needle

Superstition Mountains

PHOENIX 34

80 to 89

60 80 89

↙ FLORENCE JUNCTION 16

Weaver's Needle 4553'

⅄ camp sites
π picnic sites

Along the Apache Trail

The Superstition Mountains
loomed above Apache Junction,
their profile familiar to all
who know Arizona.
First Water Road took
me to a hiking point in the
Superstition wilderness.

I hiked to the top of a
ridge (watching for snakes)
to get a view
of Weaver's Needle.
The silence of the wilderness
was intense, interrupted
only by occasional "moo's"
from approaching
range cattle.

Weaver's Needle,
Superstition Mountains

Horse Mesa,
Apache Trail

I was impressed with the beauty of the landscape along
the Apache Trail and sketched the great view of Horse
Mesa above Fish Creek. So many lichens grew
over the great rock mass that it had a
yellowish-greenish cast in the
afternoon light.

The road to Tonto

Past Roosevelt, the tallest masonry dam in the world, and south a bit toward Globe, is Tonto National Monument. I traveled on foot up to see the ancient Salado Indian houses built around 1300 AD.

In my drawing you can see an original roof construction. At the six-foot height a large main beam was placed across the room with smaller cross-beams placed on top. Reeds or saguaro ribs were next, then mud.

Arrange in advance to see the more extensive Upper Ruin. It is larger, a longer hike, and you must be accompanied by a ranger.

As I sketched, I thought of the Salados who had been here fitting their lives to what the desert provided.

A hive of bees hummed overhead, their droning alternating with squeaking of swifts as they flew back and forth.

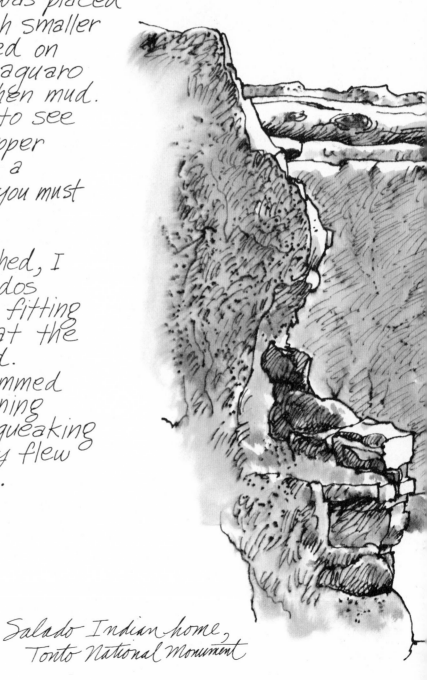

Salado Indian home,
Tonto National Monument

88

Back road to Young and the
Mogollon Rim

This was a scenic trip from
desert terrain to ponderosa pine
forests atop the Mogollon Rim and
Sitgreaves National Forest. At the
little town of Young I noticed in the
graveyard next to the Baptist Church
the headstones of people killed
in the "Pleasant Valley War", 1887. It
was a most serious shooting
feud between sheep-and
cattle-raisers.

Baptist Church at Young

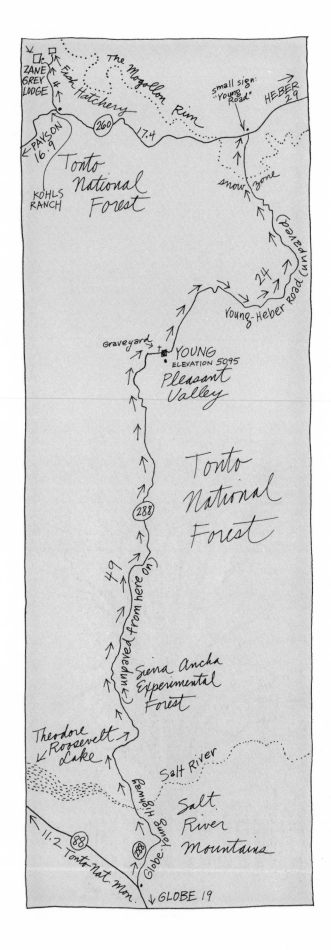

The road to Zane Grey Lodge

In the woods beneath the Mogollon (Tonto) Rim, Zane Grey built a lodge. Now open to visitors, this was his home in the western wilderness for several months each year in the 1920's. Grey wrote "Under the Tonto Rim" and many other popular novels based on knowledge and lore he gained here and in other parts of the west.

As I sketched Zane's trunk, with snarling Javalina head mounted above, the woman attendant entertained me by whistling softly over and over, "It's a _Long_ Way to Tipperary."

Just beyond here was the Tonto Creek Fish Hatchery developing trout for Arizona's forest streams.

The director told me that children visitors sometimes ask, incredulously, "Where did you ever catch all those fish?" Actually, the eggs were flown from Boston and hatched here.

This hatchery was a 1936 Works Project Administration accomplishment.

At Zane Grey Lodge under the Tonto Rim

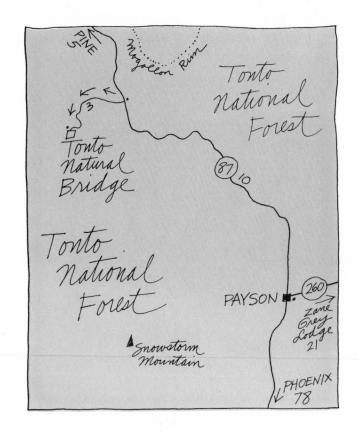

Road to the Valley of the Tonto Natural Bridge

This astonishing natural formation was first seen by white men in 1877. It was well hidden from view in a deep valley. I positioned myself with a bit of difficulty along the steep descent and, while sketching, contemplated the spring water falling from the rim of the bridge, a rainbow shining in its mist. Past the deep darkness under the arch, bright sunlight reflected on dripping travertine deposits.

There was also an intriguing wet cave along Pine Creek, but the path was not easily navigated. To reach this ask locally for directions.

Desert Deer Weed

Tonto Natural Bridge

Sunrise dancers and singers,
San Carlos Indians

Back road across the White River and the Black River

It was my good fortune to see the San Carlos Indian Sunrise Dances in a meadow along this road. An announcer stated that tape recordings of the sacred ceremony were forbidden, but pictures were permitted.

I quickly took out pen and paper and, peering over many shoulders, sketched the two graceful lead dancers. Men, young and old, chanted rhythmically in the background, while a great circle of people moved in time to the music.

It was a colorful and engrossing performance to observe on that crisp September morning.

↑SHOW LOW 53

Fort apache
Indian
Reservation

↖ HWY 60 77 14   Kinishba Ruins 🏛   WHITERIVER 4

FORT APACHE

5.6   73 ↗ CANYON DAY   3.3

General Crook's Quarters

Geronimo Cave 7.4

Salt River

3.1   77 60

Great views of Salt River Canyon

6.1 (unpaved road)

6.5

White River

SIGN: "ACCESS PERMIT, FEE REQUIRED." (does not apply to tourists)

Sycamore Reservoir

GLOBE 27

San Carlos Indian Reservation

Martin Luther Tank

Turtle Tank

road too rough here for low-slung passenger cars

Black River

Fort apache Indian Reservation

sketch of Sunrise Dancers

(unpaved road) 14.1

SAWMILL

BADLY DAMAGED SIGN: Black River 19

Gimme Tank

WEATHERED SIGN: Black River 12

17.1

NOTE: THIS IS A 43.8 MILE TRIP ON UNPAVED ROADS. SEVERAL PLACES DIFFICULT FOR ORDINARY PASSENGER CARS.

○Baskin Tank

↓SAN CARLOS 22

SAN CARLOS 22

The road went through rolling grass country, in and out of deep canyons and through stands of junipers and pines. Sturdy bridges crossed the White and the Black Rivers. A bit further downstream these two rivers joined to form the great Salt River.

The Black River

Fort Apache

At Fort Apache I saw a historic quadrangle of venerable buildings, many still in use. The old fort had been established in 1870 to help deal with marauding Apaches.

I sketched the former quarters of General George Crook, who was in charge of operations at the time. Indian boys wrestled and played nearby, gathering now and then to watch me draw. To my consternation they discussed my progress in the Apache tongue.

General Crook's quarters,
Apache museum and craft center

101

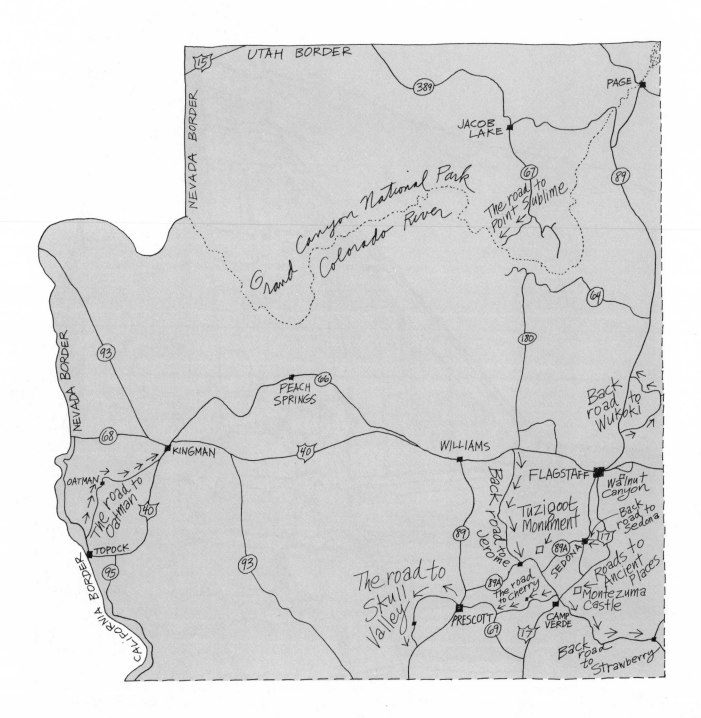

Northwestern Arizona

Northwest Arizona, like the other quadrants, holds for me more memories, associations and pleasures anticipated than I can possibly reduce to a pageful of words. There by the river—*the* river of the Southwest,—at Needles and Topock, I had my first glimpse of Arizona's irreducible wonders. There at the border I hopped my first freight train and yonder at Flagstaff, ten hours later, I spent my first night in jail for vagrancy. Vagrancy! Indeed I was guilty. A vagrant all my life, I am content to have the desert sky for my roof, the distant mountains for my only tolerable walls, the earth beneath all the floor I want or desire. Let me wander the Southwest till the end of my days, never hold title to a single square foot of real estate —*unreal* estate!—and you will not hear me complain of homelessness. The desert is my home. The mountain is my home. The river is my home. The trees are my friends, the rocks my neighbors, the dark birds soaring against the sky my wisest counselors. These quiet folk do not return my love, but they have never betrayed it either. And when I want some human companionship, which I sometimes do, I return to the town, the city, where they live, those people like me, and share for a while the best that humans can share: talk, ideas, art, a good meal, our children, our requited loves, our trails into the past, our circuits through the present, our linkages to the future. This, I think, offers what is truly most valuable in the American West: here men and women and children can still enjoy the best of both worlds—the world of the human, the world of the pre-human. Civilization *and* wilderness. That is what we must preserve: both. To save what is good, to risk only what is unnecessary. The thoughtful conservative is always a conservationist.

Prickly poppy

The road
to Oatman

Wandering burros
watched me as I sketched
the old theatre at the former mining
town of Oatman. A wild rabbit
bounded over my large feet. But
most dramatic was the setting
of the town within rugged
mountain terrain. The towering
"Elephant's Tooth" gleams white
above the town.

LAS VEGAS 102 ↖ (93)
KINGMAN
4.5 ASH
FORK
112

Battleship
Mountain

Thimble
Mountain

23.3

OATMAN
2.7 ▲ Elephant's
Tooth
3666'

Oatman Road

Oatman-Topock Highway (paved)

22.4

Davis Dam

Black Mountains

YUCCA ■

(66)

Havasu
National
Wildlife
Refuge

(40)

CALIFORNIA BORDER

• TOPOCK

← NEEDLES 14 (95)

Elephant's Tooth and the old theatre, Oatman

106

Jerome

Back road to Jerome

The trip went through ponderosa pine country to begin with. Leaving the forest, there were meadows to traverse and long views to contemplate.

Without running off, a coyote watched my vehicle pass.

At Jerome, dwellings clung to steep hillsides terraced with narrow streets and buckling sidewalks.

I sketched from above the main street, the sights and sounds of the revived mining town filling my ears and eyes.

GRAND CANYON 59

64

FLAGSTAFF 31

40   66
     89   WILLIAMS

ASH FORK 18

"SIGN: PERKINSVILLE WHITE HORSE LAKE"

8.2

Kaibab National Forest

WHITE HORSE LAKE 10

WILLIAMS TO JEROME 47.9

(paved road)

19

pavement ends

SIGN: "JEROME 22"

Prescott National Forest

Verde River

6.0

PERKINSVILLE (no town - just a ranch)

Road 354

(unpaved road)

stay on Road 318 to Jerome

Road 155

CHINO VALLEY 24

7.6

JEROME

CLARKDALE 5.4

Road 318A

6.7

ALT. 89

PRESCOTT 31

107

Tuzigoot

In the Verde Valley, not far from Jerome,
I visited the ruins of the ancient Sinagua
Indian town of Tuzigoot.

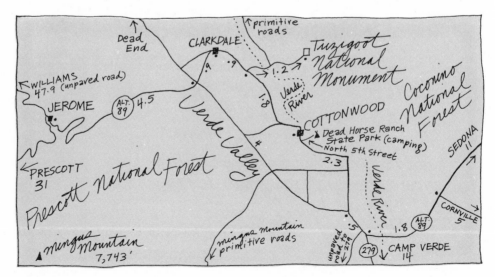

It was abandoned by the Sinagua
civilization in the 1400's. In 1933 and
1934 Tuzigoot (the Apache word for "crooked
water") was excavated by the University of
Arizona and is now a fascinating place
for all to see.

Montezuma's
Castle

Roads to ancient places

I was able to see pit house ruins
along this road showing the foundations
of a prehistoric Indian dwelling.
The large limestone sink,
Montezuma Well, was also
of great interest.
Montezuma Castle,
highlight of the drive, was
marvelous to gaze at,
so well preserved are these
houses of long ago.
I sketched while a large
raven flew in and out of the ruin
looking in swallow and dove
nests for eggs.

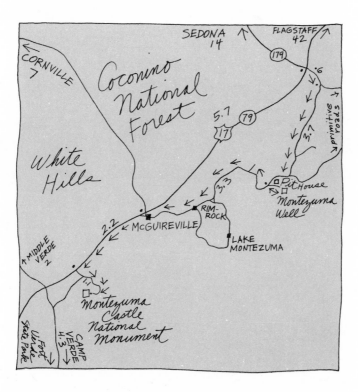

The road to Cherry

Up and up this road went with views of rolling brushland and prickly pear cactus changing to a landscape of piñon pine and juniper forest at higher elevations. There were long views back toward Sedona and the San Francisco Mountains.

The small hamlet of Cherry lay in a canyon shaded with oak and Arizona walnut trees. Wildflowers were abundant on this day in late September.

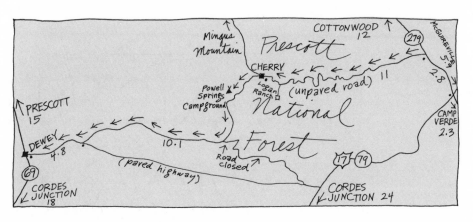

Pestemon

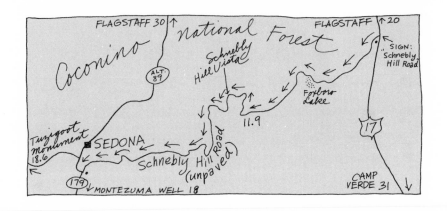

Back road to Sedona

The brilliance of thousands of goldeneye wildflowers yellowed the hillsides of the Coconino National Forest along Schnebley Hill Road. At the crest along this scenic back road views begin of the blushing-red cliffs surrounding Sedona.

Indian paint brush

Goldeneye

The road to Skull Valley

Along this road out of Prescott there was pine forest, then rolling brushland and far-reaching views of pigmy forest. In Skull Valley cows grazed in the shade of giant cottonwood trees.

In town I sketched neat and well-cared-for Skull Valley Store, obviously the meeting place for valley residents. Ask here how the valley got its name.

As long as I was there an old gent sat in front chewing tobacco. I asked him later if things had changed much in the valley in the last twenty years. He chewed a bit, then came the answer..."Nope."

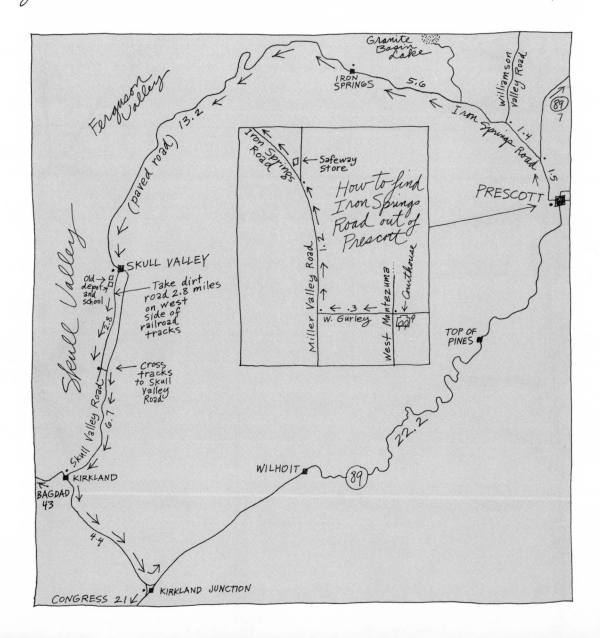

115

The road to Spring Valley

This was a gravel road over flat terrain through eye-pleasing meadows and forests. I sketched a small farm and barn along the way, with Sitgreaves Mountain at my back.

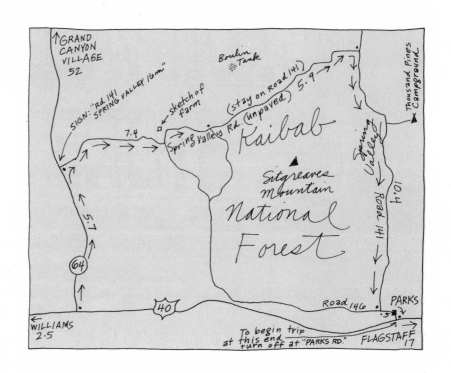

↑ GRAND CANYON VILLAGE 52

SIGN: "rd 141 SPRING VALLEY 16mi"

Boulin Tank

□ sketch of farm

(stay on Road 141)

Spring Valley Rd. (unpaved)

Thousand Pines Campground

7.4

5.9

Kaibab

Sitgreaves Mountain ▲

National Forest

5.7

64

Spring Valley

Road 141   10.4

40

Road 146

PARKS
.5

WILLIAMS 2.5

To begin trip at this end turn off at "PARKS RD."

FLAGSTAFF 17

Farm on Spring Mountain Road

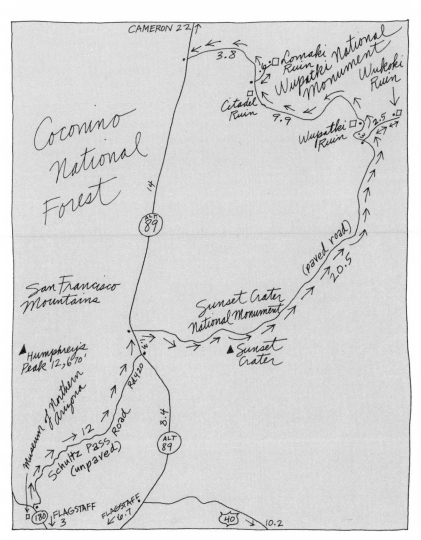

CAMERON 22

Coconino National Forest

Lomaki National Ruin

Wupatki National Monument

Wukoki Ruin

Citadel Ruin 9.9

Wupatki Ruin 2.5

ALT 89 14

3.8

San Francisco Mountains

(paved road) 20.5

Sunset Crater National Monument

▲ Sunset Crater

▲ Humphrey's Peak 12,670'

Museum of Northern Arizona

Rd 420

Schultz Pass Road (unpaved) 12

1.3

8.4

ALT 89

180 FLAGSTAFF 3

FLAGSTAFF ← 6.7

40 10.2

Schultz Pass
back road
to Wukoki

In the 1100's Wukoki
was built using the plentiful Moenkopi sandstone of
the area. The ruin of Wukoki's tower house is still
there in the high desert, strong testimony to the
considerable masonry skills of the Sinagua
Indians.   No wind blew on the day I
was there. The air
was crisp. Desert
bushes were
blooming with
white and yellow
flowers, and
Wukoki looked
splendid.

Wukoki

Back road to Walnut Canyon

I took the delightful hike along the ledges of Walnut Canyon to see the many prehistoric cliff dwellings built into the recesses of limestone canyon walls. It was a good place to live back in the 13th century for plenty of water ran through the canyon then, and fuel was abundant. Dwellings along the canyon walls were difficult for enemies to attack, rain and snow could not fall on the homes, and there was fertile soil for growing of crops above the canyon rim.

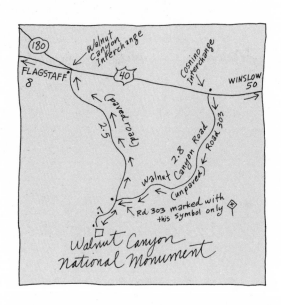

Cliff dwellings at Walnut Canyon

aspens along the
road to Point Sublime

122

The road to Point Sublime

It was a somewhat bumpy road at times, but the glory of the aspen and conifer and the astonishing color and immensity of the Grand Canyon at Point Sublime made the long trip worthwhile. And to stand on the rim alone to see such a colossal work of nature was truly a "sublime" experience.

On my return I sketched this scene along the road as little gusts of wind plucked yellow and orange leaves from the aspen trees and showered them on me and on the forest floor.

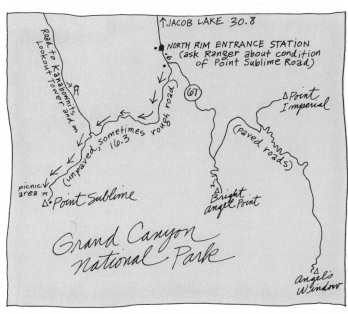

↑JACOB LAKE 30.8

NORTH RIM ENTRANCE STATION
(ask Ranger about condition of Point Sublime Road)

Road to Kanabownits Lookout Tower and on

(unpaved, sometimes rough road) 16.3

67

△Point Imperial

(paved roads)

picnic area ⌂ △·Point Sublime

△Bright angel Point

Grand Canyon National Park

△Angel's Window

Needle Rock

CAMP VERDE
← SIGN: "PAYSON"

Ranger Station
(ask about Childs road to Strawberry)

8.1

SIGN: "CHILDS"

(unpaved road) 13.9

Needle Rock

Hackberry Basin

Coconino National Forest

34 Zane Grey Highway (paved)

oldest standing public school in Arizona

87 6.5
WINSLOW 70

Irving Power Plant (unpaved road) 9.8

2.4

Childs Power Plant
5

STRAWBERRY

Tonto National Forest

PAYSON 17

Back road to Strawberry

Here was a road of desert mountain scenery, of catclaw, mesquite, prickly pear cactus and ocotillo. In Hackberry Basin I sketched the highly colored "Needle Rock." Mountains were ahead and I drove toward them sensing the magnitude of the upward thrust of the Mogollon Rim, that massive two-hundred-mile-long escarpment across much of Arizona's northland.

125

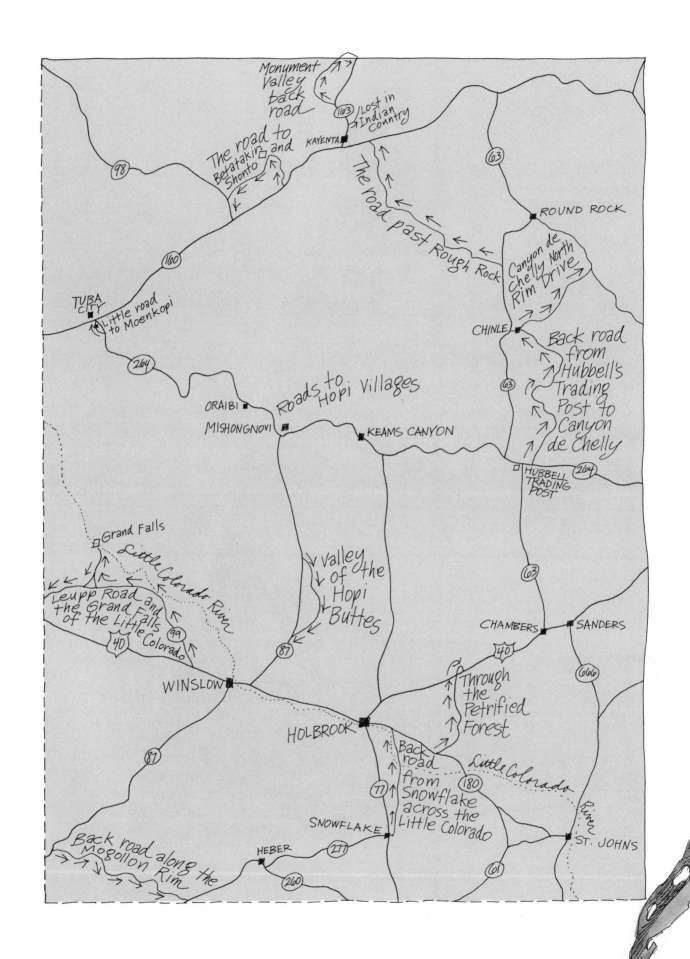

Monument
Valley
back
road

163

Lost in
Indian
Country

KAYENTA

The road to
Betatakin and
Shonto

98

160

63

ROUND ROCK

The road past Rough Rock

Canyon de Chelly North Rim Drive

TUBA
CITY

Little road
to Moenkopi

264

CHINLE

Back road
from
Hubbell's
Trading
Post to
Canyon
de Chelly

63

ORAIBI

Roads to Hopi Villages

MISHONGNOVI

KEAMS CANYON

HUBBELL
TRADING
POST

264

Grand Falls

Little Colorado River

Leupp Road and
the Grand Falls
of the Little
Colorado

99

40

Valley
of the
Hopi
Buttes

63

CHAMBERS

SANDERS

40

666

WINSLOW

87

87

Through
the
Petrified
Forest

HOLBROOK

Back
road
from
Snowflake
across the
Little Colorado

Little Colorado

180

77

River

SNOWFLAKE

ST. JOHNS

Back road along the
Mogollon Rim

HEBER

277

260

61

Northeastern arizona

Sunflower

Indian country. At this point it is traditional to say something nice about our noble red-skinned brothers and sisters. The *native* Americans, as they now choose to call themselves. But the nicest thing an honest man can say is that they are no worse than the rest of us. And no better. Like white folks, the Indians of Arizona are a complex mixture of good and bad, pretty and ugly, normal, abnormal, mediocre, indifferent. They are human like us, a bunch of unique and irreplaceable individuals, sometimes funny, sometimes tragic, equally confused. They are artists and craftsmen, laborers and politicians, rodeo cowboys and brown-skinned rednecks, strong, sick, adaptable and unadapted. Contrary to myth, the Indians are not natural ecologists or ethnic conservationists. No lands in all of the Southwest are more overgrazed, burnt-out and abused than those on the reservations. But whose fault is this? The truth is that the Indian culture was destroyed, largely obliterated, long ago by the overwhelming power of Anglo-American culture. Only remnants of it remain, pockets of traditionalism on the Hopi mesas, artifacts and ceremonies of the picturesque trotted out now and then for the benefit of the tourist trade. But having lost most of their own culture, the Indians have not been assimilated to ours. They remain stranded between the two worlds. Why mention such disagreeable facts? Why not conclude these little essays with sentiments uplifting and hopeful, leading to repose? Well, I had meant to do it—but simple reporting got in the way. Art composes, clarifies and enlightens; journalism only irritates and annoys. But that is and always has been the major difference between journalism and art.

Back road along the Mogollon Rim

The road was a bit bumpy, so I took it
easy through the cool conifer forest at the
7,000-foot level of the Mogollon Rim.
   Clean, white trunks of stately aspen
occasionally caught my eyes in the dense
forest contrasting with the dark colors
of pines and firs.
   I sketched a vast landscape of
trees and ridges from one of
the Rim viewpoints.

View from the Rim

129

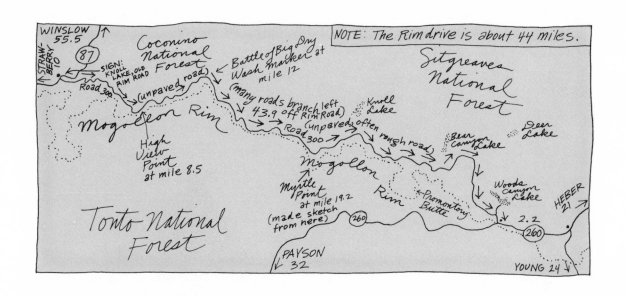

NOTE: The Rim drive is about 44 miles.

WINSLOW 55.5
STRAW-BERRY 10
87
SIGN: KNOLL LAKE, OLD RIM ROAD
Road 300
Coconino National Forest
(unpaved road)
Battle of Big Dry Wash marker at mile 12
(many roads branch left 43.9 off Rim Road)
Road 300
(unpaved, often rough road)
Knoll Lake
Mogollon Rim
Sitgreaves National Forest
Bear Canyon Lake
Deer Lake
High View Point at mile 8.5
Mogollon Rim
Myrtle Point at mile 19.2 (made sketch from here)
260
Promontory Butte
Woods Canyon Lake
2.2
260
HEBER 21
Tonto National Forest
PAYSON 32
YOUNG 24

Leupp Road and the Grand Falls of the Little Colorado

The treeless desert stretched to the horizon ahead. Grass was sparse on the red earth, although cattle and horses grazed. Always there was a view of the distant San Francisco Mountains.

Past Leupp, black lava beds and craters made the landscape more interesting.

On the way to Grand Falls I stopped to sketch this windmill and watertank. Attracted by my pickup truck several herds of multicolored horses galloped down a dusty cinder hill.

The water tank pump had broken down temporarily and they could only stand and wait.

To find the Little Colorado River here on seemingly flat, unbroken desert was a surprise! The Grand Falls would be a spectacular sight if one arrived at the proper time after a good rain. You could then bring lunch and enjoy the view, from one of the shaded picnic tables, of the then flowing Little Colorado River.

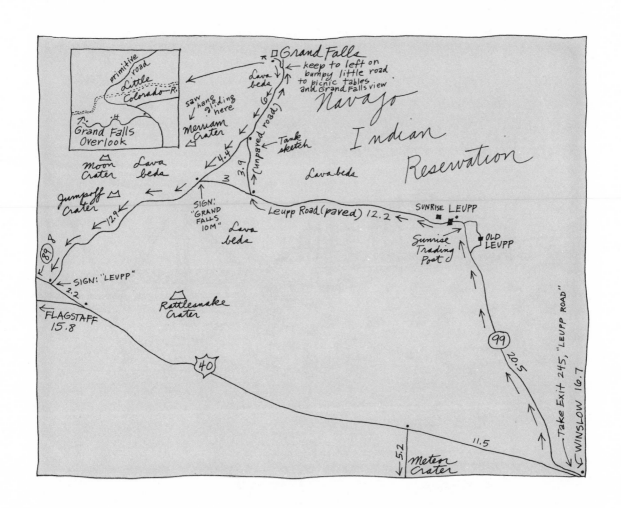

□ Grand Falls
keep to left on
bumpy little road
to picnic tables
and Grand Falls view

primitive road
Little
Colorado R.

Lava beds

saw hang gliding here

Merriam Crater

Tank sketch

(Unpaved road)

Navajo

Indian

Reservation

Lavabeds

Grand Falls Overlook

Moon Crater   Lava beds

Jumpoff Crater

SIGN: "GRAND FALLS 10M"

Lava beds

Leupp Road (paved) 12.2

SUNRISE LEUPP

Sunrise Trading Post

OLD LEUPP

12.9

89

SIGN: "LEUPP"

2.2

FLAGSTAFF 15.8

Rattlesnake Crater

40

99

20.5

Take Exit 245, "LEUPP ROAD"

WINSLOW 16.7

5.2   Meteor Crater

11.5

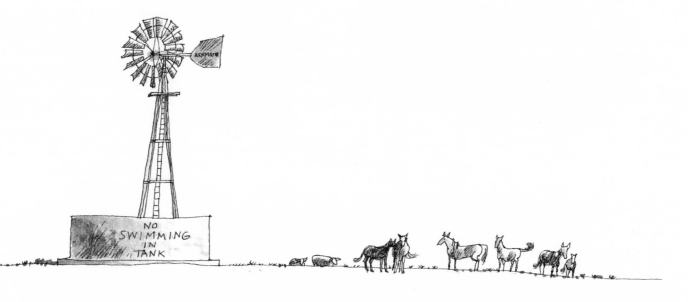

AERMOTOR

NO
SWIMMING
IN
TANK

Back road from Snowflake across the Little Colorado

The road from Snowflake went through open pastureland, and cows
  and calves often stationed themselves directly in the middle of
the road. I approached the large creatures very slowly,
  because they can move in the most unlikely direction.
Sometimes they would choose to gallop along ahead
    as if it were round-up time.

Bridge across the Little Colorado River

There is a sign on the bridge across the Little Colorado which gave me pause. It read, "Load Limit 8 tons, Bridge unsafe for trucks-cars, Cross at own risk." I crossed, then was reassured as a truck and trailer with a full load of hay also rumbled over the rusty bridge.

Eventually I reached Woodruff, a quiet farm community shaded by Lombardy poplars.

HOLBROOK
5 (180)
PETRIFIED FOREST 20.5
"Carr Lake Draw"
8.0
1.5
Woodruff Butte
WOODRUFF
keep to right
sketch of bridge
1.1
SIGN "REIMER FARMS"
(unpaved road) 14.9
77
17.5
Back road, SNOWFLAKE TO HOLBROOK, 29.5 miles
HAY HOLLOW
SNOWFLAKE
← HEBER 28
(217)
1.2
"Woodruff Turnoff"
SHOW LOW 18.8

Through the Petrified Forest

I began my trip through this painted land at the Rainbow Forest Museum by making a sketch of a very expressive big cat petroglyph.

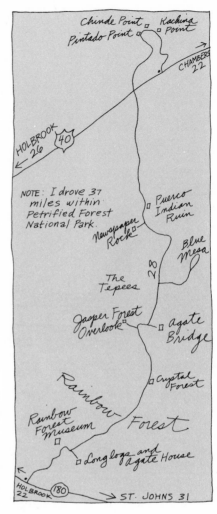

NOTE: I drove 37 miles within Petrified Forest National Park.

Big cat petroglyph

DEAR RANGER
I AM sorry I
TOOK THIS ROCK.
I WANT Other
PEOPle To see
It Too.

Petrified wood is not to be carried
off from the forest by visitors.
   Inevitably, however, small pieces are
pocketed by some children, later
  discovered by parents, then returned
to Forest Headquarters by mail with
accompanying letters of apology.
   I copied one of the letters at the
museum's "confession counter"
  for you to see.

Atop Blue Mesa I was pleased to observe a herd of pronghorn antelope grazing.

In the canyon, petrified logs sit atop small ridges until they fall, undercut by the effects of wind and water. I sketched an erosion-wrinkled hill with its log cap. Portions of the log had long ago tumbled from their perch as erosion had proceeded.

At points Pintado, Chinde and Kachina were the most colorful, exciting and extensive desert views I had ever seen.

Petrified forest at Blue Mesa

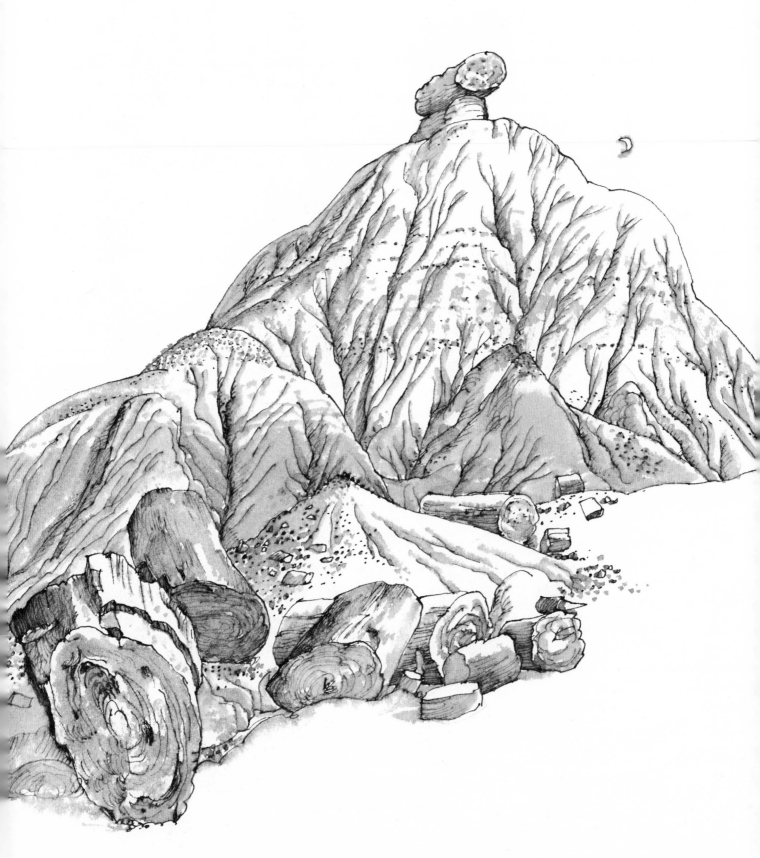

137

Elizabeth,
Navajo weaver

Back road from
Hubbell's Trading Post
to Canyon de Chelly

In the over-100-year-old
trading post I sketched
Elizabeth busily creating
a Navajo rug.
   She complained that my
picturization made her look
older than she was, and
I meekly apologized
for my "futuristic"
interpretation.

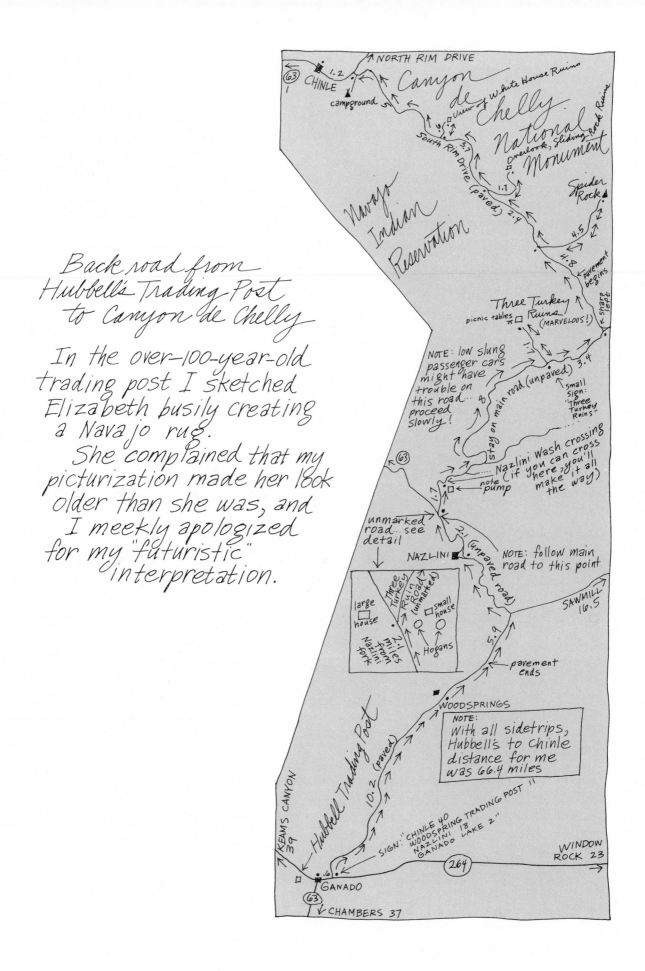

Entrance to Hubbell's Trading Post

I sketched the main entrance to Hubbell's
with its sagging screen door and leather handle.
An elderly Indian gentleman sat on a heavy
wooden bench by the door. He wore a dark
brown shirt, hat and jacket, all which showed off
to good effect the elegant turquoise and
silver jewelry he wore around his neck,
wrists and fingers.
The road to Canyon de Chelly
was bumpy and slow. Making it over
Nazlini Wash, to begin with, was the
most crucial, the rest of the trip being
manageable. There was great visual reward,
however, in viewing Three Turkey Ruin from the
Tribal Park across the gorge.
No one else came while I was there and
only the cry of a red-tailed hawk echoing
off the pink canyon walls disturbed the
silence. Tse Deeshzhasi Wash trickled
below past the ruin. With binoculars I
could see three turkeys painted on
the side of one of the buildings.

Three Turkey Ruins

144

Shaded by a gnarled,
time-worn juniper,
I sketched from my
high perch overlooking the
deep, multi-colored
canyon below.

Canyon de Chelly

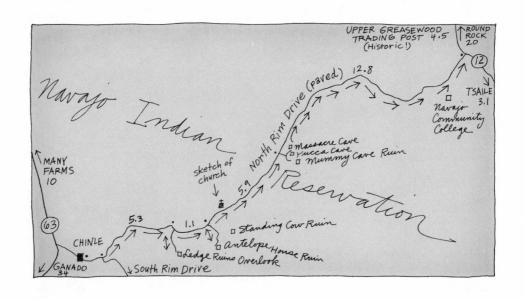

Navajo Indian Reservation

UPPER GREASEWOOD
TRADING POST 4.5
(Historic!)

↑ROUND
ROCK
20

⑫

TSAILE
3.1

Navajo
Community
College

North Rim Drive (paved) 12.8

☐ Massacre Cave
☐ Yucca Cave
☐ Mummy Cave Ruin

↑MANY
FARMS
10

sketch of
church

5.9

⑥③

5.3

CHINLE

1.1

☐ Standing Cow Ruin

Antelope House Ruin

☐ Ledge Ruins Overlook

↓GANADO
34

↓ South Rim Drive

146

Canyon de Chelly North Rim Drive

  There were overlook views of the great canyon off the main road at various points. I began watching out for tarantulas which, by their size, were quite visible as they crossed the road.

  Past Antelope House Ruin I sketched a little pink church with junipers all around. Indian ladies passed by in brightly colored dresses.

Navajo church

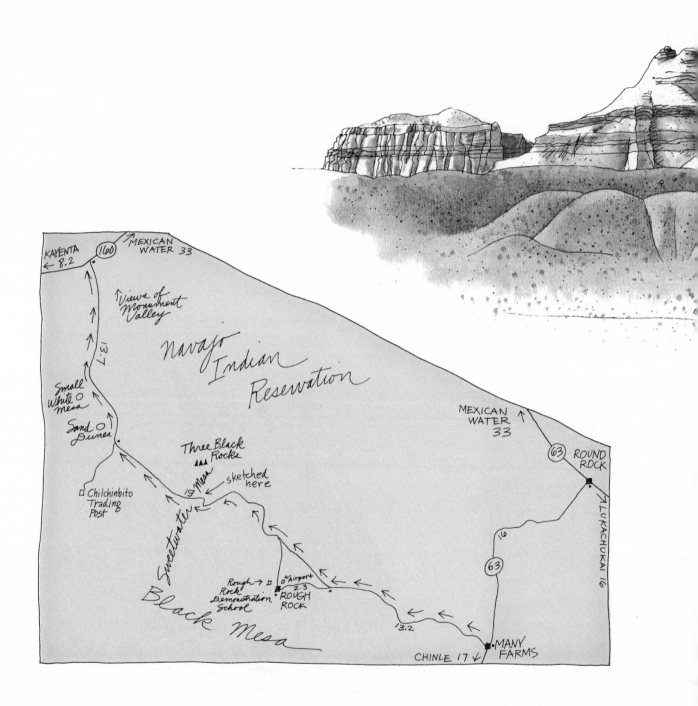

KAYENTA
← 8.2

160

MEXICAN
WATER 33

Views of
Monument
Valley

13.7

Navajo Indian
Reservation

Small
White Mesa

Sand
Dunes

Three Black
Rocks
▲▲▲

sketched
here

Mesa

Sweetwater

□ Chilchinbito
Trading
Post

Black   Mesa

Rough → □
Rock
Demonstration
School

□ Airport
• 2.3
ROUGH
ROCK

MEXICAN
WATER
33

63 ROUND
ROCK

LUKACHUKAI 16

16

63

13.2

CHINLE 17 ↓

MANY
FARMS

The road past Rough Rock

This journey was through a
land of big and little mesas,
sand dunes and strangely
shaped rocks and buttes.
It was a scenic approach
to Monument Valley, its
picturesque land
formations silhouetted
in the distance.

Sweetwater Mesa

Lost in Indian country

I got myself lost in Monument Valley on a
little back road which skirted the east
side of El Capitan. No matter which way
I chose to go, the road would end in front
of a sturdy Navajo dwelling.
        Retracing my way back to the main
road I stopped to make a drawing of
El Capitan and Owl Rock.
        The Rock resembled an owl
            from many
                points of viewing.

Navajo hogan with washing out

El Capitan and Owl Rock, Monument Valley

In the quiet of this place the tinkling of
bells sounded in the distance. Finally, a herd
of sheep and goats moved into the middle
distance of my drawing for me to sketch.
The big-eared black dog escorting the
browsing animals came close to me wagging
his tail. There was very little grass to
eat, and when the fast-moving herd swerved
toward a group of hogans in the distance,
the dog trotted off after them.

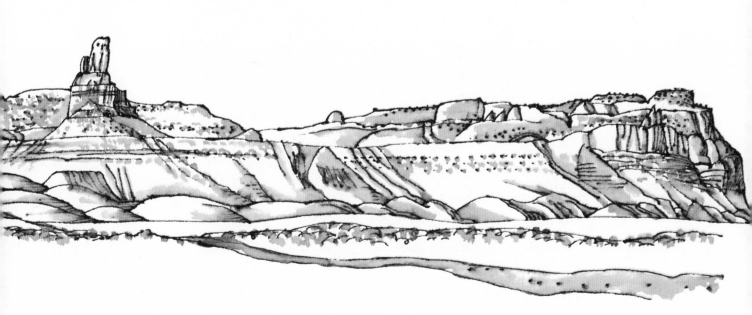

Monument Valley back road

    The road toward Hoskinnini Mesa proved more successful than the last valley road I had selected. This one followed an Indian school bus route paralleling the main road through Monument Valley.

    At the abandoned Moonlight Trading Post I took a little dirt road east and sketched this long view, East and West Mitten Rocks dark on the horizon. When I finished, a young Navajo in a tall, black cowboy hat came by in his pickup truck yelling, "Follow my dust!"

    I did, ending up at the Monument Valley highway again just a bit north of the Arizona border.

Monument Valley

The map shows:

Dead End ↑

SIGN: "Harry Gouldings Monument Valley Lodge"

UTAH BORDER

GOULDINGS ■ 5 →

Look hard for this little road .2 mile past trading post

2.3 ↗ pump house

Moonlight Trading Post (closed)

↑ sketch of Monument Valley from here

2.4

cross El Capitan Wash →

□ 8 tank and windmill

(unpaved road) 5.9

163

Navaho Indian Reservation

Monument Valley

MEXICAN HAT 25

Burnt Mesa

3.2 ←

Lost in Indian country

SIGN: "HOSKINNINI MESA NARROW CANYON"

Hoskinnini Mesa

▲ El Capitan

Owl Rock

10.6 KAYENTA ↓

The road to Betatakin and Shonto

A fast, paved road took me to the Navajo National Monument and Betatakin. At the end of a quarter-mile trail walk was the overlook of the ancient ruins.

Ravens flew by at eye level in the pink and red canyon. I thought that Betatakin, in its cozy, canyon wall recess, was like an exquisite piece of architectural jewelry.

Betatakin

Next to the Visitor Center at
Navajo National Monument was this forked-
stick hogan, an example of the earliest style
of Navajo dwelling. Three poles interlock with
forked ends at the top. More poles are laid
side by side, then covered with bark and dirt.
The doorway faces the rising sun.
   The back road to the Navajo canyon
town of Shonto had stretches of travel
over "slip rock", a large exposed
                    rock face. There
                    were also some
                    slippery sand passages.
                    It proved an adventurous
                    journey!

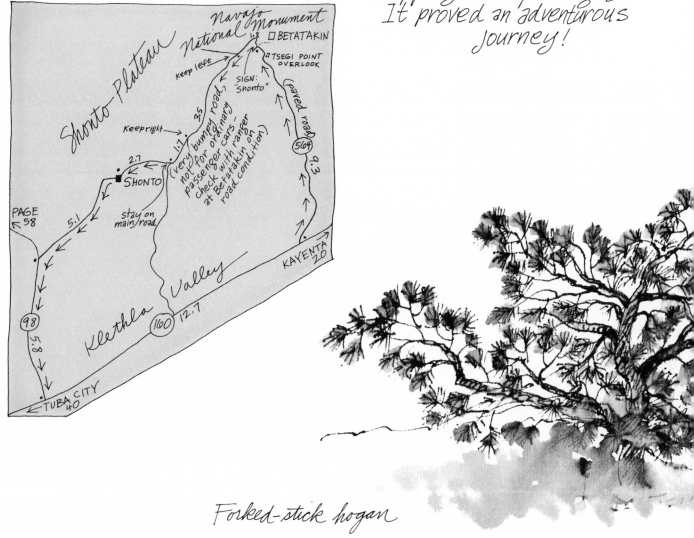

Forked-stick hogan

*Little back
road to Moenkopi*

Through a red-walled canyon
on a dirt road, past corn
crops, fenced with crooked
fence posts, this short back
road finally climbed up a
steep, rutty grade into the
small stone village
of Moenkopi.

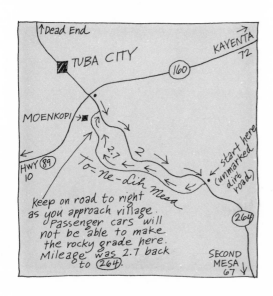

Huhuwa Kachina doll

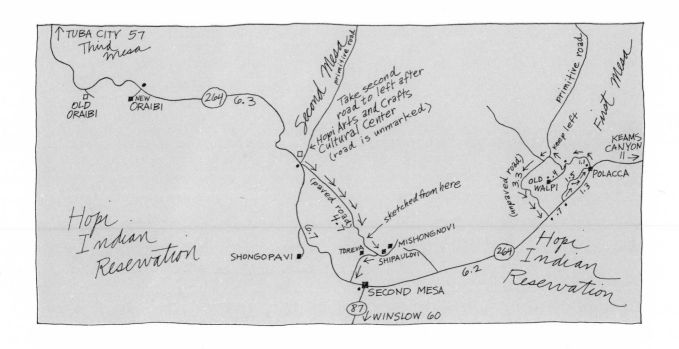

The map shows:
- TUBA CITY 57, Third Mesa (upper left, with up arrow)
- OLD ORAIBI
- NEW ORAIBI
- 264, 6.3
- Second Mesa, primitive road
- Take second road to left after Hopi Arts and Crafts Cultural Center (road is unmarked)
- sketched from here
- First Mesa, primitive road
- KEAMS CANYON 11
- keep left
- (unpaved road) 3.3
- OLD WALPI .4
- 1.1
- 1.5
- POLACCA
- 1.3
- .7
- (paved road) 4.7
- 6.1
- Hopi Indian Reservation
- SHONGOPAVI
- TOREVA
- SHIPAULOVI
- MISHONGNOVI
- 264
- Hopi Indian Reservation
- SECOND MESA
- 6.2
- 87, WINSLOW 60

Roads to Hopi Villages

Here is the story of Huhuwa, Kachina doll from one of the Hopi villages.

"Years ago, in the village of Mishongnovi, a child was born with his legs completely crossed at the knees. As he grew up he learned to overcome this handicap so successfully that he became an active worker in the fields, a good hunter, and was also quick to help anyone in the village. Moreover he was so intelligent, cheerful and kind in spite of his handicap that his life became a legend."

(Doll and legend courtesy of The Museum of Northern Arizona, Flagstaff)

Rock daisy

161

Hopi villages, Mishongnovi and Shipaulovi

The Hopi villages are
private places and I was
careful not to disturb this
privacy in my inspection of the
little mesa towns.
I sketched Mishongnovi and
Shipaulovi from a distance, the stone
architecture of these Second Mesa towns
almost indistinguishable from the
surrounding rock. This was also true of old
Walpi high up on the First Mesa.
The back road down from Walpi furnished
a unique profile of this ancient stone
town perched miraculously on the
narrow mesa top.

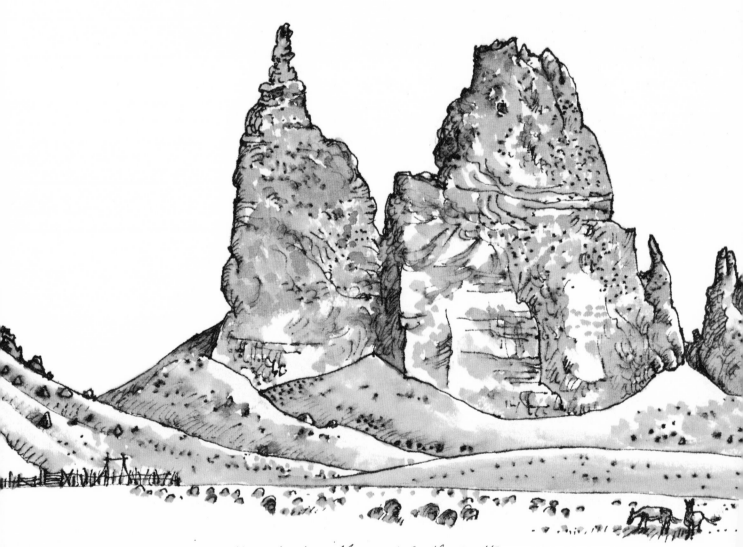

Hopi Buttes at the village of Castle Butte

164

Valley of the Hopi Buttes

The sun was low in the west when I drove
through the valley. Long shadows strengthened
the forms of the Hopi Buttes. Flat, pointed,
rounded, small or massive, they gave pleasing
variety to the landscape.

My drawing was made in the light of the
following morning. It is only a small sampling of
what there is to see in this monumental land.

I must confess that one butte was
omitted from the background. There
were just too many buttes!

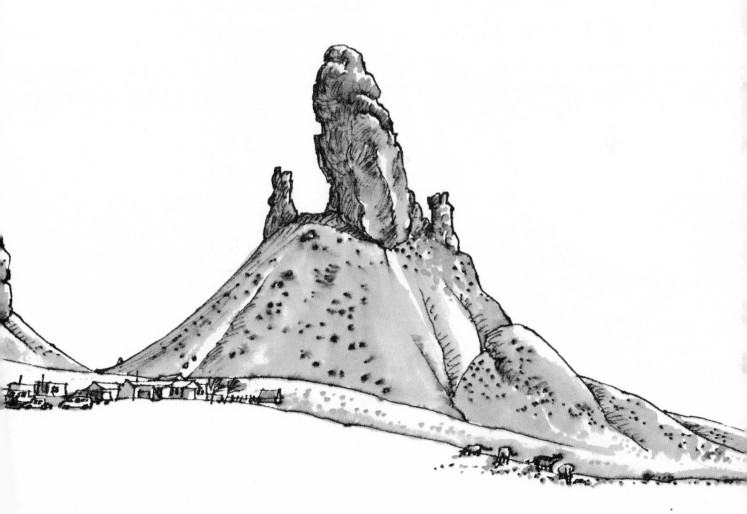

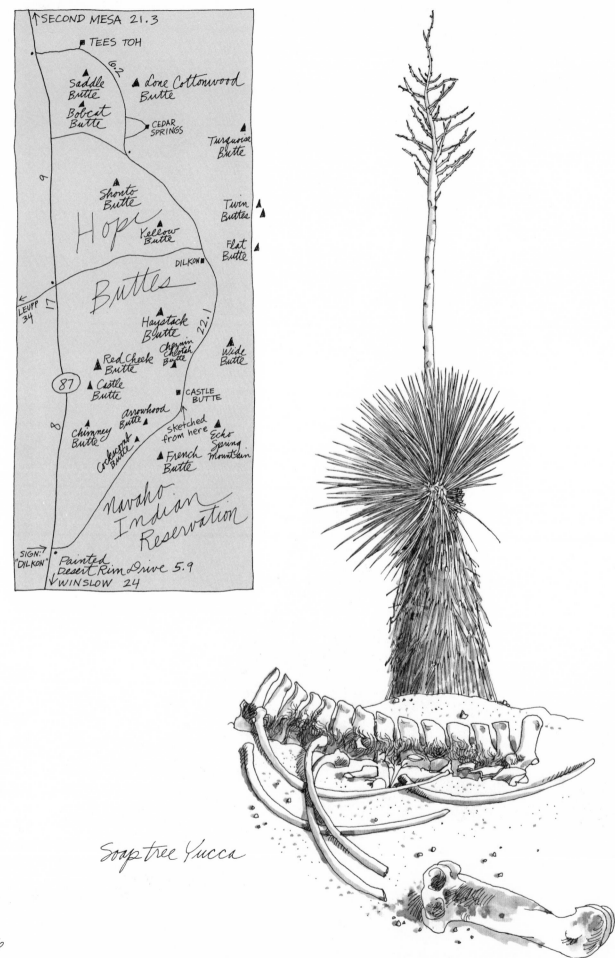

SECOND MESA 21.3

TEES TOH

Saddle Butte

Lone Cottonwood Butte

Bobcat Butte

CEDAR SPRINGS

Turquoise Butte

Shonto Butte

Hopi

Twin Buttes

Yellow Butte

Flat Butte

DILKON

Buttes

Haystack Butte

Chermin Chlotch Butte

Red Cheek Butte

Wide Butte

87

Castle Butte

CASTLE BUTTE

Arrowhood Butte

Chimney Butte

Sketched from here

Echo Spring Mountain

Cockscomb Butte

French Butte

Navaho Indian Reservation

LEUPP 34

17

SIGN: "DILKON"

Painted Desert Rim Drive 5.9

WINSLOW 24

Soap tree Yucca

Epilogue

"I see, smell, taste, hear, feel, that everlasting something to which we are allied, at once our maker, our abode, our destiny, our very selves, the one historic truth, the most remarkable fact which can become the distinct and uninvited subject of our thought, the actual glory of the universe: the only fact which a human being cannot avoid recognizing, or in some way forget or dispense with.

We need pray for no higher heaven than the pure senses can furnish, a purely sensuous life — for certainly there is a life of the mind above the wants of the body, and independent of it... such as no human institutions give out, — the early morning fragrance of the world, antedeluvian, strength and hope imparting. They who scent it can never faint... Nature, the earth herself, is the only panacea."

Henry David Thoreau
(1817–1862)

In making the drawings for Back Roads of
  Arizona I used three pens.
One was made of a section of bamboo
fashioned by myself. I would dip the
sharpened point in india ink for black
lines and in water for halftone lines.
        Another was a Rapidograph pen for
black india ink with number "oo" penpoint.
        The third pen was a broad-nibbed
Mont Blanc fountain pen filled with
"exceptionally black" Osmiroid ink. Sable hair
brushes were used for washes of grey or acrylic
color.   I worked with a variety of papers.
All drawings were completed on location.

stellar jay

For their help, patience and good
humor during travels on Arizona's
  back roads, I am indebted to
the artist, Joe Seney, and
    to my son, Wes.